WHAT PEOPLE ARE SAYING ABOUT
PENTECOST: THIS STORY IS OUR STORY . . .

"Robert Menzies offers in this book one of the clearest arguments, as well as capable support, for the classical Pentecostal position. Many outsiders to the movement may be surprised what a strong case can be made for the position. This work is compelling, nuanced, exegetically strong, and offers many new insights that both Pentecostals and non-Pentecostals can learn from."

—CRAIG S. KEENER, PhD
Professor of New Testament, Asbury Theological Seminary

"The international Pentecostal Movement not only celebrated its centennial in 2000, but launched itself into its second century. But all is not well. There has arisen a new generation within the Movement who do not know the Spirit, nor the work which He has done. Many of these are now eagerly listening to competing voices: charismatic, evangelical, emergent, and Young Calvinist. In this context some Pentecostals are now asking, "Why am I a Pentecostal?" Into this confused context Robert Menzies, writing in the lucid, irenic style for which he is well-known, explains Pentecost. His answer for the uncertain and the confused is a skillful melding of sound hermeneutics, solid exegesis, and heartfelt testimony. *Pentecost* demonstrates that Pentecostal theology and experience is by far the best twenty-first century expression of Luke's distinctive vision of the Spirit-baptized church in mission."

—ROGER STRONSTAD
Professor in Bible and Theology, "Scholar in Residence" (2011), Summit Pacific College

"Robert Menzies has provided, to date, the definitive biblical and theological apologetic for Pentecostal identity. This classical Pentecostal manifesto is informed by a vital witness to the apostolic message lived on both sides of the world. It is thus also a heartfelt invitation to other Christians—evangelicals and beyond—to be open to a new filling of the Holy Spirit of Jesus so He can continue to do immeasurably more for and through mere human beings than any of us can ask or even imagine!"

—AMOS YONG, PHD
Dean and J. Rodman Williams Professor of Theology,
Regent University School of Divinity, Virginia Beach, Virginia

"Robert Menzies continues to distinguish himself as a most capable apologist for Pentecostal theology. Pentecostal readers will find solid biblical evidence for their experience of the baptism in the Spirit; they will also be challenged to think expansively about some matters related to Spirit baptism and other Pentecostal phenomena. Non-Pentecostal readers who are open-minded and open-hearted will be compelled to give due consideration to the author's firmly based presentation of the biblical evidence."

—ANTHONY D. PALMA, THD
Professor Emeritus and Former Dean of the Theology Division,
Assemblies of God Theological Seminary

"Robert Menzies has given us a superb exposition of the biblical basis for classical Pentecostal faith. It is a persuasive apology for utilization of Luke/Acts in formulating a vital doctrine of baptism in the Holy Spirit. Its implications for life and ministry around the world are enormous."

—EDGAR R. LEE, STD
Chair, Commission on Doctrinal Purity, Assemblies of God, USA
Academic Dean Emeritus, Assemblies of God Theological Seminary

"Menzies suggests that issues like subsequence (Spirit baptism as distinct from regeneration) and initial evidence (speaking in tongues as the evidence of Spirit baptism) are not incidental but rather key to the historical development of Pentecostal theology. In making this claim, Menzies swims against the stream of more recent theological proposals concerning what is most distinctive to Pentecostal theology. His clear and well-argued position must be taken seriously by all sides of this important discussion. I highly recommend this book."

—FRANK D. MACCHIA, THD
Professor of Systematic Theology, Vanguard University

PENTECOST

THIS STORY IS **OUR** STORY

ROBERT P. MENZIES

Published by Gospel Publishing House
1445 North Boonville Avenue
Springfield, Missouri 65802

Interior typesetting by Prodigy Pixel (www.prodigypixel.com)

ISBN: 978-1-60731-341-0
Printed in the United States of America

16 15 14 • 2 3 4

Dedicated to the memory of my father,
William W. Menzies,
July 1, 1931–August 15, 2011,
a pioneer in Pentecostal theology.

CONTENTS

FOREWORD

On April 18, 1906, a reporter for *The Los Angeles Times* wrote a front-page story about a church service he had attended the previous night. Titled, "Weird Babel of Tongues," the reporter opened with these words: "Breathing strange utterances and mouthing a creed which it would seem no sane mortal could understand, the newest religious sect has started in Los Angeles." He was writing about the Azusa Street Mission.

Azusa Street was neither new nor sectarian, however. The revival traced its roots to Acts 2, where the outpouring of the Holy Spirit upon the disciples had similarly resulted in speaking in tongues, mockery from the crowds, and the bold proclamation of the gospel. Just as the first Pentecost was an inclusive event, representative of "every nation under heaven" (Acts 2:5), so Azusa Street was interracial and trans-denominational. In both cases—Pentecost and Azusa Street—the gospel of Jesus Christ and the gift of the Holy Spirit were free for all.

There is one other similar element between the first Pentecost and Azusa Street. Both employed what you might call a this-is-that hermeneutic. Peter explained to the mocking Jerusalem crowd what was happening among the disciples: "this is that which was spoken by the prophet Joel" (Acts 2:16, KJV). Just so, Azusa Street in effect said, "This is that which happened in the book of Acts." This fusion of horizons between biblical promise and contemporary experience is characteristic of Pentecostals worldwide.

Indeed, according to Bob Menzies, it is what defines Pentecostalism. As he tells it, a Pentecostal is simply "a Christian who believes that the book of Acts provides a model for the contemporary church" (p. 13). The experience of the first Pentecostal believers is the same experience as the current generation of Pentecostal believers. Their story is our story.

It's because Pentecostals fuse the biblical and contemporary horizons that we link baptism in the Holy Spirit with speaking in tongues, since that's what Acts 2 does. It's why we associate Spirit-baptism with empowerment for mission rather than with spiritual regeneration. And it's why we expect God to perform "signs and wonders" and to manifest spiritual gifts in worship services. All these things happened in the first Pentecostal community, and their story is our story.

The book you hold in your hands explains and defends the Pentecostal understanding of Spirit-baptism through a careful reading of the relevant New Testament evidence. Bob Menzies is a Pentecostal believer, Assemblies of God minister, New Testament scholar, and personal friend. I pray that this book will inform you, but I also pray that it will inspire you to seek more "power" from the Holy Spirit so that you can be a better "witness" to Jesus Christ both at home and abroad (Acts 1:8).

On April 18, 1906, a 7.9-magnitude earthquake rocked San Francisco, California, knocking Azusa Street off the front page of the next day's *The Los Angeles Times.* The earthquake was a big deal, of course. But as we look back on the twentieth century, we see clearly that it was the worldwide growth of Pentecostalism that really "turned the world upside down" (Acts 17:6, KJV). As we look forward into the twenty-first century, may our story as Pentecostals continue to be theirs in ever-increasing measure!

GEORGE O. WOOD
General Superintendent, Assemblies of God
Chairman, World Assemblies of God Fellowship

PREFACE

Many friends and colleagues helped make the publication of this book possible. First and foremost, I would like to thank my brother, Glen Menzies, for his help in writing my father's Life Summary (the Appendix). It was a joy to work with Glen as together we reflected back on the many interesting, inspiring, and at times, humorous events that marked significant milestones in our father's life. Glen's ability to remember specific details truly amazed me. While the Life Summary was a collaborative work, Glen's role was most significant. Much of this material was presented orally at our father's funeral, which was conducted at Central Assembly of God in Springfield, Missouri on August 20, 2011. Glen and I also presented this material in a modified form at the twentieth annual William W. Menzies Lectureship, which convened at Asia Pacific Theological Seminary in Baguio City, the Philippines from January 30 through February 3, 2012.

I would also like to thank my friends, Grant Hochman, Robert Graves, Edgar Lee, Anthony Palma, and Roger Stronstad, each of whom read the manuscript in its entirety and offered helpful comments. While these men should not be held responsible for any of the book's shortcomings, their input certainly enhanced the final product.

I would also like to thank a special group of ministers and scholars in Taiwan and Hong Kong: Joshua Iap, Solomon Wong, Timothy Yeung, and Aaron Zhuang. I have been encouraged and inspired by my interaction with these dear friends. I consider the hours I've spent discussing various aspects of Pentecostal theology with them a rare gift.

Perhaps I should mention a group of friends in mainland China, but I fear that they are too numerous to mention. Let me just say that the past eighteen years have been far richer than I could have imagined. I have learned more from this dedicated group than words can express.

Steve Blount and Terri Gibbs of Assemblies of God Publishing have been extremely helpful and encouraging. I would like to thank them both for adding their expertise and skill to this project.

Three chapters in this book were originally presented as special lectures in Amsterdam, Hong Kong, and Taipei. In Amsterdam, I was asked by the Free University, in conjunction with the Assemblies of God Bible School that is housed there, to present a Pentecostal perspective on baptism in the Holy Spirit at a Theological Symposium on Pentecostal Theology (February, 2005). This was the genesis of Chapter Two. A slightly adapted version of this lecture was later published in the *Journal of Pentecostal Theology* and is used here with permission.[1] I was also asked by the Taiwan Assemblies of God to present two special lectures on the role of tongues in the New Testament at the second annual Chinese Conference on Pentecostal Theology, which convened in Taipei, September 27–29, 2011. These lectures formed the basis of Chapter Three, although they were originally presented in Chinese. A modified English version of these lectures was presented at the twentieth annual William W. Menzies Lectureship noted above. Finally, in Hong Kong on October 24, 2011, I was privileged to present a paper on Pentecostal hermeneutics at a symposium for a group of Evangelical pastors and teachers sponsored by Ecclesia Bible College, an Assemblies of God school. This lecture formed the basis for Chapter One.

---

1   Robert Menzies, "Luke's Understanding of Baptism in the Holy Spirit: A Pentecostal Dialogue with the Reformed Tradition," *Journal of Pentecostal Theology* 16 (2008): 1–16.

I should also note that Chapter Four incorporates material from my review of Keith Hacking's book in *The Evangelical Quarterly:* "A Review of 'Signs and Wonders, Then and Now: Miracle-working, Commissioning and Discipleship' by Keith J. Hacking," *Evangelical Quarterly* (2007), 261–65. This material is used with permission.

I would like to thank the various schools, churches, and journals noted above for their invitations to speak and write on topics that are significant for the Pentecostal movement and indeed, as I argue below, for the larger body of Christ. I believe that the international nature of these groups accurately reflects the global impact of the modern Pentecostal movement.

INTRODUCTION

A few months ago a good friend asked me, "Why do Pentecostals talk so much about baptism in the Holy Spirit?" He wanted to know what stimulated Pentecostals to emphasize this specific spiritual experience. My response surprised him. I simply suggested that he should read the second chapter of the book of Acts. Although this may come as a surprise to some, Pentecostal experience and practice is driven and shaped by the Bible, particularly the narrative of Acts. It is impossible to understand Pentecostals apart from this basic, fundamental fact.

Sadly, today many seek to do exactly this. In fact, many academics scoff at the notion that we can identify with any precision who Pentecostals are.[2] Indeed, the idea that we can define Pentecostals theologically is often ridiculed.[3] Why is this the case? When we have a relatively clear understanding of what it means to be a Presbyterian, a Lutheran, or a Methodist, and all of these definitions or identity markers center on theological affirmations, why should it be so difficult to define what it means to be a Pentecostal?

---

2   Note for example the incredibly broad definition offered by Allan Anderson in *Spreading Fires: The Missionary Nature of Early Pentecostalism* (Maryknoll, NY: Orbis, 2007), 4: "Pentecostalism . . . is a polynucleated and variegated phenomenon. . . . It is best seen from its pneumatological centre as historically related movements where the emphasis is on the exercise of spiritual gifts." See also Allan Anderson, *An Introduction to Pentecostalism: Global Charismatic Christianity* (Cambridge: Cambridge University Press, 2004), 9–15.

3   Allan Anderson suggests that global Pentecostals generally are not concerned about doctrine but rather with experience and the practice of spiritual gifts (*Introduction*, 14). He suggests a broad definition for Pentecostalism so that he can avoid "the bigotry of excluding those who do not agree with a particular understanding of the Bible" (*Introduction*, 10).

In fact, it is not. There is general agreement that the origins of the modern Pentecostal movement can be traced back to January 1, 1901, and a little Bible school in Topeka, Kansas. There, a clear connection was made between the experience of baptism in the Holy Spirit and speaking in tongues. This experience was understood in the light of the description of the miraculous outpouring of the Spirit on the Day of Pentecost that is described in Acts 2 as an enabling for mission.[4] This theological perspective— that the experiences described in Acts should serve as a model for contemporary Christian experience, that the baptism in the Holy Spirit (Acts 2:4) is a post-conversion enabling for mission, and that speaking in tongues marks this experience—was transmitted to William Seymour, an earnest black preacher who brought the Pentecostal message to a small, makeshift mission in Southern California. The Azusa Street revival (1906–1909) that Seymour presided over sowed the seeds of a movement that would grow into what one scholar has termed "the most successful social movement of the past century."[5] As a result of this revival, the Pentecostal message that the power that animated the apostolic church is available today was taken around the world.

Of course there were other revival movements featuring the work of the Spirit that occurred either shortly before or after the Azusa Street revival in various parts of the world. Some of the revivals included manifestations such as speaking in tongues. However, none of these other revival movements produced a clear message like the revival at Azusa Street. None of these other revival movements presented tongues as the biblical sign

---

4   Some Pentecostals, particularly those connected with the Holiness tradition, understand this empowering to enhance other dimensions of the Christian life as well.

5   Philip Jenkins, *The Next Christendom: The Coming of Global Christianity* (Oxford: Oxford University Press, 2003), 8.

of baptism in the Holy Spirit (Acts 2:4). This was an important symbol, a key part of that clear message that was taken around the globe. We shall explore the importance of this connection between tongues and Spirit baptism in the following chapters. For now, it is sufficient to recognize that the Azusa Street revival was, in this sense, unique and for this reason it had a unique impact.[6] The events that took place in that small Bible school in Topeka, Kansas, and which blossomed in the Azusa Street revival, represent the beginning of a connected history, the birth of the Pentecostal movement. The Azusa Street revival, then, is rightly considered by most scholars to be the key catalyst for the modern Pentecostal movement.

If the origins and the central doctrines of the Pentecostal movement are relatively clear, why is it so difficult for scholars to identify or define what it means to be a Pentecostal? I believe that there are pragmatic and ideological reasons for the reluctance within the academic community to define Pentecostals theologically and with precision.

The pragmatic reason has to do with the fact that many, particularly those holding teaching or research positions in universities, want to describe the Pentecostal movement in the largest and broadest terms possible. Huge numbers produce excitement, interest, and, ultimately, funding for research. To be fair to those engaged in sociological research, we must also acknowledge that researchers often intentionally strive to understand and describe broad trends in society. The focus on Pentecostal and charismatic Christianity in the largest possible terms is often an extension of their different aims and purposes,

---

6   Vinson Synan concludes: "It is unthinkable that the Pentecostal movement could have developed as it did without the initial evidence position" (V. Synan, "The Role of Tongues as Initial Evidence" in *Spirit and Renewal: Essays in Honor of J. Rodman Williams,* ed. Mark Wilson [Sheffield: Sheffield Academic Press, 1994], 67–82; quote from 82).

which generally focus on illuminating cultural trends, and are not directly related to the life of the church.

It is also true that church leaders are not immune from the desire to describe the movement they are associated with in the largest possible terms. Additionally, many Christian leaders, particularly those who desire to stress the ecumenical significance of the Pentecostal movement, are reluctant to define the movement in clear, theological language. While precise definitions bring clarity, they also establish limits. They form markers that help shape identity, but these markers also exclude. Simply put, when it comes to describing Pentecostals, many like broad, fuzzy definitions because they are inclusive and lead to enormous numbers. But if everyone is a Pentecostal, then what does this term mean?

It is certainly true that the Pentecostal movement has spawned other groups and what sixty years ago was, at least in theological terms, a relatively homogeneous movement has become much more diverse and produced many splinter movements in recent years.[7] Nevertheless, there are many theological descriptions that may be used to define other groupings of Christians in relation to Pentecostals. I would like to suggest the following definitions as both historically accurate and helpful for our present discussion:

---

7   Although early Pentecostals differed on many issues, there was widespread acceptance of the three tenets noted below. These three tenets distinguished and unified the movement: (1) that the experiences described in Acts should serve as a model for contemporary Christian experience (thus gifts of the Spirit were seen as currently available); (2) that the baptism in the Holy Spirit (Acts 2:4) is a post-conversion enabling for mission (some also connected this experience to broader elements of the Christian's life); and (3) that speaking in tongues marks this experience. Even the early leaders in the Charismatic movement embraced this theological perspective. Vinson Synan, for example, shows how Charismatics "such as Harald Bredesen, Dennis Bennett, Howard Ervin, and Rodman Williams, differed in only minor ways from their Pentecostal brethren on the question of tongues as evidence" (Synan, "Role of Tongues," 75–76).

Pentecostal: a Christian who believes that the book of Acts provides a model for the contemporary church and, on this basis, encourages every believer to experience a baptism in the Spirit (Acts 2:4), understood as an empowering for mission, distinct from regeneration, that is marked by speaking in tongues, and affirms that "signs and wonders," including all of the gifts listed in 1 Corinthians 12:8–10, are to characterize the life of the church today.

Neo-Pentecostal: a Christian who agrees and acts in accordance with all of the tenets listed above except the affirmation that speaking in tongues serves as a normative sign for Spirit baptism.

Charismatic: a Christian who believes that all of the gifts listed in 1 Corinthians 12:8–10, including prophecy, tongues, and healing, are available for the church today; but rejects the affirmation that baptism in the Spirit (Acts 2:4) is an empowering for mission distinct from regeneration.

Non-Charismatic: a Christian who rejects the affirmation that baptism in the Spirit (Acts 2:4) is an empowering for mission distinct from regeneration, and who also rejects the validity of at least one or more of the gifts of the Spirit listed in 1 Corinthians 12:8–10 for the church today.

It should be noted that all of the categories listed above are compatible with the term *Evangelical*. With the designation

Evangelical, I refer to those Christians who affirm: the authority of the Bible; that salvation is found only in Christ; and that evangelism is thus an important part of the Christian's mission in the world.

The global Pentecostal movement is firmly rooted in Evangelical soil, a fact that far too many contemporary scholars are unwilling to admit. It is impossible to understand Pentecostals apart from these core Evangelical convictions. At its heart, the Pentecostal movement is not Spirit-centered but Christ-centered. The work of the Spirit, as Pentecostals understand it, centers on exalting and bearing witness to the Lordship of Christ. Pentecostals echo the apostolic message: Jesus is Lord. Jesus is the One who baptizes in the Spirit. Additionally, it should be noted that Pentecostal faith and practice flow from the Bible. Pentecostals are often pictured as extremely emotional and experientially driven, but this is a caricature of the real image. In reality, Pentecostals are "people of the Book." Although Pentecostals certainly encourage spiritual experience, they do so with a constant eye to Scripture. As I have noted, the Bible, and particularly the book of Acts, fosters and shapes Pentecostal experience. The movement started in a Bible school and was stimulated by careful study of the Bible. The Christ-centered and Bible-driven nature of the Pentecostal movement should not be missed.

Yet, again, this is often the case.[8] The reason for this is that many scholars studying the movement, generally not practicing Pentecostals themselves, seek to define the Pentecostal movement largely or exclusively in sociological

---

8   An Evangelical seminary professor in Hong Kong recently asked me with genuine concern if Pentecostals were growing hostile to the Evangelical movement. He cited the tone and content of a number of publications associated with the Society for Pentecostal Studies as the reason for his concern. I assured him that the vast majority of grassroots Pentecostals strongly identified with Evangelical values.

terms.[9] In a detached manner they identify Pentecostals not by what they believe, but rather by the nature of their experience (e.g., Do they exercise spiritual gifts?)[10] or their behavior (e.g., What differences can we observe in the lives of Pentecostal believers?)[11] While sociological analysis can provide many helpful insights, on its own it cannot fully comprehend or adequately describe this profoundly Christ-centered and Bible-based movement. This is particularly true when sociological analysis is consciously driven by ideological concerns. For example, a post-colonial reading of Pentecostal history may reject the Azusa Street revival as the epicenter of the movement because of its location in the United States. The core theological tenets that I have described might also be rejected as the products of the Western and colonial mind, in spite of the fact that Pentecostals around the world base their experience and practice on the same biblical texts, make the same or similar affirmations, and proclaim the same risen Lord.[12] In short, sociological analysis can only take us so far and it often comes

---

9   See, for example, Harvey Cox, *Fire from Heaven: The Rise of Pentecostal Spirituality and the Reshaping of Religion in the Twenty-first Century* (Cambridge, MA: Da Capo Press, 2001 [originally published in 1995]). Cox consistently minimizes the biblical and Christ-centered nature of the movement. See also Donald E. Miller and Tetsunao Yamamori, *Global Pentecostalism: The New Face of Christian Social Engagement* (Berkeley: University of California Press, 2007). This book is interesting and informative; however, in my opinion, it tells us little about Pentecostals and more about the agenda of the authors and general trends within the larger evangelical community. Additionally, the potential perils of the "progressive" Pentecostals' social activism are not adequately addressed. Why should Pentecostals embrace a missiological approach that has not served the mainline churches well?

10   Anderson, *Introduction*, 14.

11   For example, David Martin highlights the significant social impact that Pentecostals are making in Latin America by helping people rise out of poverty and by empowering women (see *Tongues of Fire: The Explosion of Protestantism in Latin America* [Oxford: Basil Blackwell, 1990]).

12   Allan Anderson's generally insightful writings, cited above, may be criticized for at times offering a biased, post-colonial reading of the evidence.

with a lot of baggage. More positively, we must recognize that sociological tools and analysis are not primarily intended or designed to meet the needs of the church.

It should not be surprising then that, as a Pentecostal, when I read sociologically-oriented books about Pentecostals, even those that contain many significant and helpful insights, I feel that something is lacking. I often feel that the picture presented of what it means to be a Pentecostal is a caricature, an image that, while partially true, contains many exaggerations and distortions. Indeed, when I read a book of this type, the one thing that I can be pretty sure of is this: the book will tell me as much about the author and his or her agenda as it does about Pentecostals and what really makes us tick, our beliefs.[13] I am tempted to write a book entitled *The Quest for the Historical Pentecostal,* and like Albert Schweitzer in his famous tome, expose the presuppositions that have shaped the caricatures that have been produced. However, as I pondered the problem, I determined to produce something more constructive.[14] This, then, is the genesis of this book.

In the pages that follow, I would like to explain why I am a Pentecostal. My definitions are unapologetically theological. My approach is thoroughly biblical. I will attempt to show how key passages in the Bible support my Pentecostal convictions. I believe that we as Pentecostals need to re-examine and clarify the rich theological legacy that the early Pentecostal pioneers have passed on to us. The reluctance to give clear, theological definition to the Pentecostal movement misses something extremely important:

---

13   Great examples of this, as I have noted above, are Miller and Yamamori's *Global Pentecostalism* and Cox's *Fire from Heaven.*

14   As Arlene M. Sanchez Walsh writes, "Better simply to get on with the work of giving my community a voice" ("Whither Pentecostal Scholarship?" *Books and Culture* [May-June 2004], 34–36; quote from 36).

it not only misses the fact that the movement was shaped by the Bible; it also loses sight of a genuine need of the church. We need to know who we are. We need to pass on the legacy.

So, let's return to the key question: What do we mean when we say, "I am a Pentecostal"? I believe that an accurate answer to this question should include three elements. First, as I have stated, Pentecostals read the book of Acts as a model for their lives. Is this appropriate and consistent with the biblical author's intention? We shall examine this question in Chapter 1. Secondly, Pentecostals emphasize that the baptism in the Spirit promised to every believer in Acts 1–2 should not be confused with regeneration or conversion; rather, it is a prophetic and missiological empowering. We shall explore the biblical evidence for this position in Chapter 2. Thirdly, I have noted that the Pentecostal movement from its inception, in accordance with the narrative in Acts (Acts 2:4; 10:46; 19:6), linked speaking in tongues with the baptism in the Holy Spirit. The early Pentecostals thus described tongues as a unique marker, a sign or evidence of baptism in the Spirit, and many historians insist that without this connection between tongues and Spirit baptism, there would be no Pentecostal movement. In Chapter 3, I seek to explain why this perspective on tongues is important for Pentecostals today and why I believe that it accurately represents Luke's intention. In Chapter 4, I take up a question that flows naturally from the Pentecostal reading of Acts as a model for our lives: Should every believer expect to see "signs and wonders" as a part of our Christian life and witness? Then, in Chapter 5, I offer my assessment of why Pentecostal churches around the world are growing at such a rapid pace.[15] Finally, in an Appendix, my brother, Glen, and I present a Life Summary of our father, William W. Menzies. Since my father passed down to us or inspired so many of the ideas presented in this book and was a life-long Pentecostal, I believe this is a particularly fitting way to conclude the book.

Whether you are a committed Pentecostal seeking to better understand your own theological heritage or a skeptical non-charismatic Christian puzzled by your rather loud neighbors, I trust you will find this book informative, challenging, and edifying. Although I cannot claim to speak for every Pentecostal, I do present the viewpoint of one who has grown up and ministered in Pentecostal churches his entire life. I am an ordained Assemblies of God minister and a practicing Pentecostal. I have also been privileged to live and minister in various countries in Asia for over twenty years and am married to the daughter of Pentecostal missionaries who served in Latin America for over forty years. Although I pursued my theological studies in broadly Evangelical settings (MDiv, Fuller Seminary; PhD, University of Aberdeen, Scotland), my commitment to Pentecostal values has not wavered. I also believe that my years of ministry in various church-based contexts have enabled me to stay in touch with Pentecostals in the pew. This encourages me in my belief that the views presented in this book will resonate well with the vast majority of grassroots Pentecostals around the world. It is my prayer that this book will encourage every reader to take up the prophetic vocation that is ours and bear bold witness for Jesus through the Holy Spirit's power.

---

15   The various chapters in this book are interrelated and build upon one another. At the same time, each chapter focuses on a specific topic. Thus, I have attempted to write each chapter so that it may also be read and understood independently. While I have attempted to keep the duplication of material to a minimum, some overlap has been necessary in order to meet this objective.

CHAPTER ONE

WHY WE READ DIFFERENTLY

We Pentecostals have always read the narrative of Acts, and particularly the account of the Pentecostal outpouring of the Holy Spirit (Acts 2), as a model for our lives. The stories of Acts are *our* stories: stories of fishermen called to bear bold witness for Jesus in the face of great opposition; stories of peasants persevering in the midst of great suffering; stories of powerful, demonic adversaries seeking to discourage and destroy. Pentecostals the world over identify with these stories, especially since so many face similar challenges.[16] This sense of connection with the text encourages us to allow the narrative to shape our lives, our

---

16   On the Pentecostal orientation of the Chinese house church movement, see Luke Wesley, *The Church in China: Persecuted, Pentecostal, and Powerful* (*Asian Journal of Pentecostal Studies* 2; Baguio: AJPS Books, 2004).

hopes and dreams, our imagination.[17] So, the stories of Acts are our stories, and we read them with expectation and eagerness: stories of the Holy Spirit's power, enabling ordinary disciples to do extraordinary things for God.

We Pentecostals have never viewed the gulf that separates our world from that of the text as large. Fusing our horizons with that of the text takes place naturally, without a lot of reflection, largely because our world and that of the text are so similar. Whereas Western theologians and scholars of the past two centuries have exerted great energy wrestling with how to interpret biblical texts that speak of God's miraculous activity, Pentecostals have not been afflicted with this sort of angst.[18] While Rudolph Bultmann developed his demythologizing approach to the New Testament,[19] Pentecostals quietly (well, perhaps not so quietly) prayed for the sick and cast out demons. As Evangelical theologians, following in the footsteps of B. B. Warfield, sought to explain why we should accept the reality of the miracles recorded in the New Testament but, at the same time, not expect them today,[20] Pentecostals were (at least in our eyes)

---

17   On the role of imagination in the hermeneutical enterprise, see Joel Green, "Learning Theological Interpretation from Luke," in *Reading Luke: Interpretation, Reflection, Formation*, eds. Craig G. Bartholomew, Joel B. Green, and Anthony Thiselton. Scripture and Hermeneutics Series, vol. 6 (Grand Rapids: Zondervan, 2005), 59.

18   Sociologist Margaret M. Poloma notes that "Ever since the famous Azusa Street Revival (1906–1909) in Los Angeles ... the Pentecostal/Charismatic (P/C) movement has battled the forces of modernity with revival fires." *Main Street Mystics: The Toronto Blessing and Reviving Pentecostalism* (Walnut Creek: AltaMira Press, 2003), 15.

19   Rudolph Bultmann, "New Testament and Mythology," in *Kerygma and Myth: A Theological Debate by Rudolf Bultmann and Five Critics*, ed. H. W. Bartsch (New York: Harper & Brothers, 1961), 1–2: "The mythical view of the world which the New Testament presupposes ... is incredible to modern man, for he is convinced that the mythical view of the world is obsolete."

20   On Benjamin Warfield's cessationist views, see Jon Ruthven, *On the Cessation of the Charismata: The Protestant Polemic on Postbiblical Miracles* (*Journal of Pentecostal Theology Supplement Series* 3; Sheffield: Sheffield Academic Press, 1993), 41–111.

witnessing Jesus perform contemporary "signs and wonders" as He established His church.

No, the hermeneutic of most Pentecostal believers is not overly complex. It is not filled with questions about historical reliability or outdated worldviews. It is not excessively reflective about theological systems, cultural distance, or literary strategies.[21] The hermeneutic of the typical Pentecostal believer is straightforward and simple: the stories in Acts are *my* stories—stories that were written to serve as models for shaping my life and experience. This is not to say that Pentecostals fail to exercise discernment or judgment. After all, not all stories are filled with the exploits of heroes. There are villains, and not every aspect of a story is to be emulated. However, the fact remains, Pentecostals have readily embraced (detractors would say, uncritically) the stories of Acts as *our* stories, stories that shape our identity, ideals, and actions.

> The hermeneutic of the typical Pentecostal believer is straightforward and simple: the stories in Acts are *my* stories—stories that were written to serve as models for shaping my life and experience.

This simple, narrative approach to the book of Acts, I believe, is one of the great strengths of the Pentecostal movement. It is undoubtedly a large reason for its rapid growth around the world. The simplicity of reading the text as a model for our lives, without angst about the miraculous or how it all fits into complex

---

21   Although this remains true at the grassroots level, there is a growing group of Pentecostal theologians and biblical scholars. Note, for example, the Society for Pentecostal Studies and its journal, *Pneuma*, as well as the *Journal of Pentecostal Theology*.

theological systems, clearly enables the message to be readily grasped by people in pre– or semi–literate cultures, people that function in more experiential and less cognitive cultures. We should not forget that these people represent the majority of the inhabitants of our planet. They, too, generally exhibit little concern about stories filled with miracles but rather readily identify with them.[22]

All of this suggests that Pentecostals have a distinctive hermeneutic, a distinctive way of reading the Bible. In this chapter, I would like to highlight how we Pentecostals read the Bible, particularly Luke-Acts, in a manner different from our non-Pentecostal Evangelical brothers and sisters. At the outset I wish to acknowledge the close link that binds Pentecostals and Evangelicals together. Indeed, Pentecostals generally identify themselves as Evangelicals (I certainly do) and in many parts of the world Pentecostals represent the majority of Evangelicals in their region. (As a matter of convenience, throughout this book I will often refer to Pentecostals and Evangelicals as distinct groups, yet it should be noted that by these terms I simply denote Pentecostal Evangelicals on the one hand and non-Pentecostal Evangelicals on the other.) Pentecostals are Evangelicals in the sense that we affirm the authority of the Bible; proclaim that salvation is found only in Jesus (Acts 4:12); and thus emphasize the importance of sharing the gospel with others. Additionally, in many respects, most Pentecostals read the Bible in a manner similar to our Evangelical brothers and sisters. Pentecostals and Evangelicals stress the importance of the intent of the biblical author and seek to understand a

---

22   On several occasions, as I have translated orally the testimonies of Chinese believers for visitors to China from Western nations, I have been tempted to tone down their references to amazing supernatural occurrences for fear that their foreign visitors might think they are crazy.

passage in the light of its historical and literary context. Historical meaning is important to both groups.

In spite of these important areas of congruence, there are two (often unconscious) assumptions that shape Evangelical approaches to Luke-Acts that Pentecostals reject. The first assumption is associated with the Evangelical tendency to reject the Acts narrative and the apostolic church it describes as a model for the church today. This assumption, simply put, is that Luke wrote to provide a historical account of the beginnings of the church so that subsequent readers might have an accurate account of the gospel message and be assured of the historical basis upon which its stands. So far so good; but there is more. Evangelicals also insist that since Luke's historical narrative treats a unique era in the life of the church, it should be understood that the events he describes are not presented as models for the missionary praxis of subsequent generations of Christians.[23] In short, Evangelicals generally assume that Luke the historian wrote to provide the church with its message, not its methods.

The second assumption is an outgrowth of the Evangelical tendency to reduce New Testament theology to Pauline

---

23   See, for example, Ben Witherington III, *The Acts of the Apostles: A Socio-Rhetorical Commentary* (Grand Rapids: Eerdmans, 1998), 132; Darrell Bock, *Acts*, Baker Exegetical Commentary on the New Testament (Grand Rapids: Baker, 2007), *passim* (cf. Darrell Bock, *Luke*, The IVP Commentary Series [Downers Grove: InterVarsity Press, 1994], 189–90); and Keith J. Hacking, *Signs and Wonders, Then and Now: Miracle-Working, Commissioning, and Discipleship* (Nottingham: Apollos/IVP, 2006), *passim.* Witherington highlights the "unique" nature of Pentecost. Bock also fails to develop the theological implications of Acts 1–2 for the missionary praxis of the contemporary church (see my review of Bock's Acts commentary in *Pneuma* 30 [2008]: 349–50). Hacking argues that the miracles of Jesus and the apostles were not intended to serve as models for the post-apostolic church and that the commissioning accounts are relevant only to a select few (see my review of Hacking's book in *Evangelical Quarterly* 79 [2007]: 261–65).

theology.[24] After all, Luke is a historian and Paul, the theologian. This myopia has significantly impacted Evangelical perspectives on the work of the Spirit. Evangelicals assume that Luke's references to the reception and work of the Spirit have essentially the same meaning as similar terms used by Paul and thus should be understood in the light of these Pauline texts. The result is that Evangelicals insist that Pentecost represents the disciples' entrance into the new age, their initiation into the life of the new covenant.[25] Pentecost, we are told, is the birthday of the church.[26]

These assumptions lie behind the chorus of Evangelical scholars who, with one voice, constantly tell us that Pentecost is a unique and unrepeatable event.[27] As a young student I was puzzled by these statements. In what sense is Pentecost unique? Any event in history cannot be repeated, but many events in the narrative of Acts are clearly presented as models for Luke's church. They are recorded by Luke precisely so that they will be repeated in the lives of his readers. Why do Evangelical scholars insist that Pentecost is unique and unrepeatable? Through my

---

24   This elevation of Paul above all other canonical writers actually has its roots in the Reformation. Luther and Calvin emphasized Paul's epistles, which supported their respective doctrines of justification by faith and the sovereignty of God. However, this privileging of Paul was further encouraged by the understandable but over-reaction on the part of Evangelical scholars to German scholarship critical of the historical reliability of Acts. Thus, Evangelicals until more recently, have viewed Luke as a historian and not a theologian. For more on the Evangelical response, see William W. and Robert P. Menzies, *Spirit and Power: Foundations of Pentecostal Experience* (Grand Rapids: Zondervan, 2000), 38–42.

25   James D. G. Dunn, *Baptism in the Holy Spirit* (London: SCM Press, 1970), 43: "In terms of Luke's scheme of salvation-history all this simply means that the new age and covenant does not begin for the disciples until Pentecost."

26   Joel B. Green, *How to Read the Gospels and Acts* (Downers Grove: InterVarsity Press, 1987), 113: "Pentecost is a nonrepeatable event. Only once can the new age be ushered in and the church be given birth."

27   Dunn, *Baptism*, 53: "Pentecost can never be repeated—for the new age is here and cannot be ushered in again." Note also Witherington, *Acts*, 132: "[of Pentecost] . . . in crucial ways it is unique."

study of Luke-Acts and the related secondary literature, I began to see that the two assumptions cited above shape Evangelical attitudes at this point.

I would like to critique these assumptions, and particularly the notion that Pentecost is "unique and unrepeatable," by examining various aspects of Luke's narrative. In the process, I trust that Evangelicals and Pentecostals might come to better understand each other and why, at times, we read the Bible differently. Of course, as a Pentecostal, my hope is that my Evangelical brothers and sisters will grow in their appreciation of a Pentecostal approach to Luke-Acts.

1. THE STRUCTURE OF LUKE-ACTS

Every New Testament scholar worth his salt will tell you that Luke 4:16–30, Jesus' dramatic sermon at Nazareth, is paradigmatic for Luke's gospel. All of the major themes that will appear in the gospel are foreshadowed here: the work of the Spirit; the universality of the gospel; the grace of God; and the rejection of Jesus. And this is the one significant point where the chronology of the Gospel of Luke differs from the Gospel of Mark. Here Luke takes an event from the middle of Jesus' ministry and brings it right up front to inaugurate the ministry of Jesus. Luke does this because he understands that this event, particularly Jesus' recitation of Isaiah 61:1–2 and His declaration that this prophecy is now

> I would like to critique . . . the notion that Pentecost is "unique and unrepeatable," by examining various aspects of Luke's narrative.

being fulfilled in His ministry, provides important insights into the nature of Jesus and His mission. This passage, then, provides us with a model for Jesus' subsequent ministry.

It is interesting to note that Luke provides a similar sort of paradigmatic introduction for his second volume, the book of Acts. After the coming of the Spirit at Pentecost, Peter delivers a sermon (Acts 2:14–41) that in many ways parallels that of Jesus in Luke 4. In his sermon, Peter also refers to an Old Testament prophecy concerning the coming of the Spirit, this time Joel 2:28–32, and declares that this prophecy, too, is now being fulfilled (Acts 2:17–21). The message is clear: Just as Jesus was anointed by the Spirit to fulfill His prophetic vocation, so also Jesus' disciples have been anointed as end-time prophets to proclaim the Word of God. The text of Joel 2:28–32 that is cited here, like the paradigmatic passage in Luke 4, also shows signs of careful editing on the part of Luke.[28]

One change is especially instructive. In Acts 2:18 Luke inserts the phrase, "And they will prophesy," into the quotation from Joel.[29] This insertion simply emphasizes what is already present in the text of Joel. The previous verse has already reminded us that this end-time outpouring of the Spirit of which Joel prophesies is nothing less than a fulfillment of Moses' wish "that all the LORD's

---

28   When I refer to Luke's editorial activity, I do not in any way wish to imply that Luke's narrative is historically inaccurate. Rather, I merely wish to point out that while Luke writes history—accurate history—he does so with a theological purpose in view. Luke clearly, on occasion, summarizes the content of speeches or dialogues, and in so doing, he utilizes his own vocabulary and style as he presents this material. As we shall see, he also paraphrases Old Testament quotations in a manner that enables him to highlight important themes that run throughout his narrative. While it is my assumption that Luke's editorial work accurately reflects and emphasizes dominical and apostolic themes, the essential question that I seek to answer centers on the content of Luke's message. It is this message, after all, that I believe to be inspired by the Holy Spirit and authoritative for the church.

29   All English Scripture citations are taken from the NIV unless otherwise noted.

people were prophets" (Num. 11:29). Acts 2:17 quotes Joel 2:28 verbatim: "I will pour out my Spirit on all people. Your sons and daughters will prophesy." Now, in verse 18, Luke echoes this refrain. Luke highlights the fact that the Spirit comes as the source of prophetic inspiration because this theme will dominate his narrative. It is a message that Luke does not want his readers to miss. The church in "these last days," Luke declares, is to be a community of prophets— prophets who are called to bring the message of "salvation to the ends of the earth" (Isa. 49:6; Acts 1:8). And now Luke reminds his readers that they also have been promised power

> **Just as Jesus was anointed by the Spirit to fulfill His prophetic vocation, so also Jesus' disciples have been anointed as end-time prophets to proclaim the Word of God.**

to fulfill this calling. The Spirit will come and enable his church— Luke's and ours—to bear bold witness for Jesus in the face of opposition and persecution.

We have already noted that this theme of bold, prophetic witness is anticipated in Luke's gospel. Jesus is anointed with the Spirit so that He might "preach the good news to the poor," so that He might "proclaim freedom for the prisoners" and "proclaim the year of the LORD's favor" (Luke 4:18–19). The parallels between Jesus' experience at the Jordan and that of the disciples at Pentecost are striking and clearly intentional. Both occur at the beginning of the respective missions of Jesus and the early church, both center on the coming of the Spirit, both are described as a prophetic anointing in the context of a sermon that cites Old Testament prophecy. Through his careful shaping of the narrative, Luke presents Jesus, the ultimate prophet, as a model for all of His followers, from Pentecost onward.[30] Luke's church has a mission to carry out, a message to proclaim.

This motif of bold, Spirit-inspired witness is also highlighted in the teaching of Jesus. Luke foreshadows events that will follow in his second volume by relating the important promise of Jesus recorded in Luke 12:11–12: "When you are brought before synagogues, rulers and authorities, do not worry about how you will defend yourselves or what you will say, for the Holy Spirit will teach you at that time what you should say."

> **Just as Jesus' experience of the Spirit at the Jordan serves as a model for the experience of the disciples' on the day of Pentecost, so also the disciples' experience at Pentecost serves as a model for subsequent Christians.**

Immediately after Pentecost, in the first story Luke recounts, we begin to see how relevant and important this promise of Jesus is for the mission of the church. Luke describes the dramatic story of Peter and John's encounter with a crippled beggar, his healing, and the apostles' arrest. The Jewish leaders command the apostles to stop preaching about Jesus. But Peter and John reply with incredible boldness. They declare, "Judge for yourselves whether it is right in God's sight to obey you rather than God. We cannot help speaking about what we have seen and heard" (Acts 4:19–20).

This is merely the beginning of the persecution the end-time prophets must face. Peter and the apostles (Acts 5:29–32), Stephen

---

30   Luke 11:9–13 also indicates that Luke views the prophetic vocation of Jesus, the Twelve, and the Seventy (Luke 10:1) as applicable to his church.

(Acts 6:10; cf. 7:51–52), and Paul (Acts 9:16; 28:31) all boldly bear witness for Jesus in the face of intense opposition and persecution.

Luke's motive in presenting these models of Spirit-inspired ministry—Peter, John, Stephen, and Paul, to name a few—should not be missed. Luke has more in mind than simply declaring to his church, "This is how it all began!" Certainly Luke highlights the reliability of the apostolic witness to the resurrection of Jesus. And he wants to be sure that we are all clear about their message, which is to be handed on from generation to generation, people group to people group, until it reaches "the ends of the earth." Yet Luke also narrates the ministry of these end-time prophets because he sees them as important models of missionary praxis that his church needs to emulate. These characters in Acts demonstrate what it truly means to be a part of Joel's end-time prophetic band and thus challenge Luke's readers to fulfill their calling to be a light to the nations. As they face opposition by relying on the Holy Spirit, who enables them to bear bold witness for Jesus no matter what the cost, these end-time prophets call Luke's church to courageously follow the path first traveled by our Lord.

All of this suggests that Luke structures his narrative in order to highlight the fact that just as Jesus' experience of the Spirit at the Jordan serves as a model for the experience of the disciples' on the day of Pentecost, so also the disciples' experience at Pentecost serves as a model for subsequent Christians. This judgment is supported by Peter's words in Acts 10:47: "They have received the Holy Spirit just as we have."

2. THE SENDING OF THE SEVENTY (LUKE 10:1-16)

Let us now turn to a text unique to Luke's gospel, Luke's account of the Sending of the Seventy (Luke 10:1–16). All three synoptic gospels record Jesus' words of instruction to the Twelve as He sends them out on their mission. However, only Luke records a second, larger sending of disciples (Luke 10:1–16). In Luke 10:1 we read, "After this the LORD appointed seventy–two [some mss. read, 'seventy'] others and sent them two by two ahead of him to every town and place where he was about to go." A series of detailed instructions follow. Finally, Jesus reminds them of their authority, "He who listens to you listens to me; he who rejects you rejects me; but he who rejects me rejects him who sent me" (10:16).

A central question centers on the number of disciples that Jesus sent out and its significance. The manuscript evidence is, at this point, divided. Some manuscripts read "seventy," while others list the number as "seventy-two." Bruce Metzger, in his article on this question, noted that the external manuscript evidence is evenly divided and internal considerations are also inconclusive. Metzger thus concluded that the number "cannot be determined with confidence."[31] More recent scholarship has largely agreed with Metzger, with a majority opting cautiously for the authenticity of "seventy-two" as the more difficult reading.[32]

---

31   Bruce Metzger, "Seventy or Seventy-Two Disciples?," *New Testament Studies* 5 (1959), 299–306 (quote, 306). See also the response of Sidney Jellicoe, "St Luke and the 'Seventy (-Two)," *New Testament Studies* 6 (1960), 319–21.

32   A "more difficult reading" refers to a unique version of a text preserved in early manuscripts that is hard to explain as a scribal correction, omission, or addition. Thus, this "difficult" reading is often viewed as authentic. All of the following scholars favor the "seventy-two" reading as original: Darrell L. Bock, *Luke 9.51–24.53*, Baker Exegetical Commentary of the New Testament (Grand Rapids: Baker Academic, 1996), 994; I. Howard Marshall, *The Gospel of Luke: A Commentary on the Greek Text* (NIGCT; Grand Rapids: Eerdmans, 1978), 415; Joel Green, *The Gospel of Luke* (NICNT; Grand Rapids: Eerdmans, 1997), 409; Robert C. Tannehill, *The Narrative Unity of Luke-Acts: A Literary Interpretation, Volume 1: The Gospel According to Luke* (Philadelphia: Fortress Press, 1986), 233; Craig Evans, *Luke*, New International Biblical Commentary (Peabody: Hendrickson, 1990), 172. One exception to this general rule is John Nolland, who favors the "seventy" reading (*Luke 9.21–18.34*, Word Biblical Commentary 35B [Dallas: Word, 1993], 546).

Although we cannot determine the number with confidence, it will be important to keep the divided nature of the manuscript evidence in mind as we wrestle with the significance of this text.

Most scholars agree that the number (for convenience, we will call it "seventy") has symbolic significance. Certainly Jesus' selection of twelve disciples was no accident. The number twelve clearly symbolizes the reconstitution of Israel (Gen. 35:23–26), the people of God. This suggests that the number seventy is rooted in the Old Testament narrative and has symbolic significance as well. A number of proposals have been put forward,[33] but I would argue that the background for the reference to the "seventy" is to be found in Numbers 11:24–30. This passage describes how the Lord "took of the Spirit that was on [Moses] and put the Spirit on the seventy elders" (Num. 11:25). This resulted in the seventy elders, who had gathered around the Tent, prophesying for a short duration. However, two other elders, Eldad and Medad, did not go to the Tent; rather, they remained in the camp. But the Spirit also fell on them and they too began to prophesy and continued to do so. Joshua, hearing this news, rushed to Moses and urged him to stop them. Moses replied, "Are you jealous for my sake? I wish that all the LORD's people were prophets and that the LORD would put his Spirit on them!" (Num. 11:29).

The Numbers 11 proposal has a number of significant advantages over other explanations: (1) it accounts for the two textual traditions underlying Luke 10:1 (How many actually prophesied in Numbers 11?); (2) it finds explicit fulfillment in the narrative of Acts; (3) it ties into one of the great themes of Luke–Acts, the work of the Holy Spirit; and (4) numerous allusions to Moses and his actions in Luke's travel narrative support our

---

33   For the various options see Metzger, "Seventy or Seventy-Two Disciples?," 303–4 and Bock, *Luke 9.51–24.53*, 1015.

suggestion that the symbolism for Luke's reference to the Seventy should be found in Numbers 11.[34]

With this background in mind, the significance of the symbolism is found in the expansion of the number of disciples "sent out" into mission from the Twelve to the Seventy. The reference to the Seventy evokes memories of Moses' wish that "all the LORD's people were prophets," and, in this way, points ahead to Pentecost (Acts 2), where this wish is initially and dramatically fulfilled. This wish continues to be fulfilled throughout Acts as Luke describes the coming of the empowering Spirit of prophecy to other new centers of missionary activity, such as those gathered together in Samaria (Acts 8:14–17), Cornelius' house (Acts 10:44–48), and Ephesus (Acts 19:1–7). The reference to the Seventy, then, does not simply anticipate the mission of the church to the Gentiles; rather, it foreshadows the outpouring of the Spirit on all the servants of the Lord and their universal participation in the mission of God (Acts 2:17–18; cf. 4:31).[35]

> The reference to the Seventy . . . foreshadows the outpouring of the Spirit on all the servants of the Lord and their universal participation in the mission of God.

In Luke's view, every member of the church is called (Luke 24:45–49; Acts 1:4–8/Isa. 49:6) and empowered (Acts 2:17–21;

---

34   For more detailed support of this position, see Robert P. Menzies, *The Language of the Spirit: Interpreting and Translating Charismatic Terms* (Cleveland, TN: CPT Press, 2010), 73–82.

35   Keith F. Nickle, *Preaching the Gospel of Luke: Proclaiming God's Royal Rule* (Louisville: Westminster John Knox Press, 2000), 117: "The 'Seventy' is the church in its entirety, including Luke's own community, announcing the in-breaking of God's royal rule throughout the length and breadth of God's creation."

cf. 4:31) to be a prophet. Far from being unique and unrepeatable, Luke emphasizes that the prophetic enabling experienced by the disciples at Pentecost is available to all of God's people. Their story is indeed our story. At Pentecost, Moses' wish now begins to be realized. Luke 10:1 anticipates the fulfillment of this reality.

3. ACTS 2:17-21 AND SALVATION HISTORY

We have already noted the important role that Luke's edited version of Joel's prophecy (Acts 2:17–21) plays in Luke's narrative. One additional modification of the text from Joel is important for our discussion. Joel's text only refers to "wonders in the heavens and on the earth" (Joel 2:30). Yet Luke's skillful editorial work enables him to produce the collocation of "signs and wonders" found in Acts 2:19. By simply adding a few words, Luke transforms Joel's text so that it reads: "I will show wonders in the heaven *above*, and *signs* on the earth *below*" (Acts 2:19, emphasis added). The significance of this editorial work becomes apparent when we read the verses that immediately follow the Joel quotation. Peter declares, "Jesus . . . was a man accredited by God to you by miracles, wonders and signs" (Acts 2:22). The significance of Luke's editorial work is magnified further when we remember that Luke also associates "signs and wonders" with the ministry of the early church. In fact, nine of the sixteen occurrences of the collocation of "signs and wonders" (σημεῖα καὶ τέρατα) in the New Testament appear in the book of Acts.[36] Early in the narrative of Acts, the disciples ask the Lord to stretch out His "hand to heal and perform miraculous signs and wonders" through the name of Jesus (Acts 4:31). This prayer is answered in dramatic fashion. A few

---

36   Acts 2:19, 22, 43; 4:30; 5:12; 6:8; 7:36; 14:3; 15:12.

verses later we read, "the apostles performed many miraculous signs and wonders among the people" (Acts 5:12). Similarly, Luke describes how Stephen, one outside the apostolic circle, "did great wonders and miraculous signs among the people" (Acts 6:8). The Lord also enabled Paul and Barnabas "to do miraculous signs and wonders" (Acts 14:3; cf. 15:12).

All of this demonstrates that by skillfully reshaping Joel's prophecy, Luke links the miracles of Jesus and those of the early church together with the cosmic signs listed by Joel (Acts 2:19–20). These miraculous events are "signs and wonders" that mark these "last days." Luke, then, is not only conscious of the significant role that miracles have played in the growth of the early church, he also anticipates that these "signs and wonders" will continue to characterize the ministry of the church in our day. We, too, live in the "last days," that epoch bracketed by the first and second comings of Jesus. According to Luke, it is an era that is to be marked by signs and wonders.[37]

This text, then, demonstrates that for Luke, the salvation history presented in his narrative cannot be rigidly segmented into discrete periods. The Kingdom of God (or the new age when God's covenant promises begin to find fulfillment) is inaugurated with the miraculous birth of Jesus (or, at the very latest, with Jesus' public ministry, which was marked by miracles) and continues to be progressively realized until His second coming and the consummation of God's redemptive plan. Pentecost is indeed a significant eschatological event, but it does not represent the disciples' entrance into the new age;[38]

---

37   According to Luke, the ministry of Joel's end-time prophets will also feature divine guidance (Acts 2:17) and bold witness (Act 2:18).

38   Only by reading Luke-Acts through the lens of Pauline theology can Pentecost be construed as the moment when the disciples enter into the new age.

rather, Pentecost is the fulfillment of Moses' wish that "all the LORD's people were prophets" (Num. 11:29; cf. Joel 2:28–29 and Acts 2:17–18) and, as such, represents an equipping of the church for its divinely appointed mission. In short, in this crucial passage Luke stresses the continuity

Luke stresses the continuity that unites the story of Jesus and the story of the early church.

that unites the story of Jesus and the story of the early church. Luke's two-volume work represents the "one history of Jesus Christ,"[39] a fact that is implied by the opening words of Acts: "In my former book, Theophilus, I wrote about all that Jesus began to do and to teach . . ." (Acts 1:1).[40]

One other significant implication flows from this insight: the birthday of the church cannot be dated to Pentecost. Indeed, in his stimulating monograph, Graham Twelftree argues that, for Luke, the beginning of the church must be traced back to Jesus' selection of the Twelve. Twelftree declares, "Luke would not call Pentecost the birth of the Church. For him the origins of the Church [are] in the call and community of followers of Jesus during his ministry."[41] Furthermore, Twelftree asserts that "the ministry of the Church is not seen as distinct from but continues the ministry of Jesus. . . . "[42] These conclusions, drawn largely from Luke's portrait of the apostles, are supported by Luke's citation of Joel's prophecy.

---

39   Martin Hengel, *Acts and the History of Earliest Christianity,* trans. J. Bowden (London: SCM Press, 1979), 59.

40   Graham H. Twelftree, *People of the Spirit: Exploring Luke's View of the Church* (Grand Rapids: Baker, 2009), 30.

41   Ibid., 28.

42   Ibid.

CONCLUSION

One of the great strengths of the Pentecostal movement is that it has read the promise of Pentecost contained in Peter's quotation of Joel (Acts 2:17–21) as a model for the mission of the church. I have argued that this approach to the text, although it runs counter to many Evangelical interpretations and assumptions, captures well Luke's intent. Luke has carefully crafted his narrative and skillfully edited the quotation from Joel. A close reading reveals that Luke's narrative is much more than a nostalgic review of how it all began. Although Luke is concerned to stress the reliability of the apostolic witness, his purposes go beyond this. Luke's narrative also provides us with much more than merely a summary of apostolic preaching. Although Luke desires to affirm the content of our message, again his purposes are larger. Through his two-volume work, Luke declares that the church, by virtue of its reception of the Pentecostal gift, is nothing less than a community of prophets. It matters not whether we are young or old, male or female, rich or poor, black or white; the Spirit of Pentecost comes to enable every member of the church, each one of us, to fulfill our prophetic call to be a light to the nations.

> **Luke calls us to be attentive to the leading of the Spirit, who delights to direct us down risky and surprising roads.**

Pentecost, then, is a paradigm for the mission of the church. Far from being unique and unrepeatable, Luke anticipates that the story of Pentecost will shape the experience of every follower of Jesus. Luke speaks directly to his church and to ours. Luke calls us to be attentive to the leading of the Spirit, who delights to direct us down risky and surprising roads. Luke challenges us to bear bold witness for Jesus, irrespective of the obstacles or opposition before us, for we can rely on the power of the Spirit to sustain us and grant us strength. And Luke encourages us to expect "signs and wonders" to accompany our ministry. May our prayer be that of the early church, "LORD, . . . enable your servants to speak your word with great boldness. . . . Stretch out your hand to heal and perform miraculous signs and wonders through the name of your holy servant Jesus" (Acts 4:29–30).

BAPTISM IN THE HOLY SPIRIT

N ot long ago a Chinese house church leader commented, "When Western Christians read the book of Acts, they see in it *inspiring stories;* when Chinese believers read the book of Acts, we see in it *our lives.*" My Chinese friend's point was clear: their experience of opposition and persecution impacts how they read Luke's narrative. Chinese believers tend to read Luke-Acts with a sense of urgency and desperation, a sense of hunger generated by their need. So, they easily identify with the struggles of Peter and John, of Stephen and Paul. And so also they readily accept the promise of the Spirit's enabling to persevere and bear bold witness for Jesus in the face of opposition. Implicit in my friend's comment was also the belief that Christians in a stable and affluent West, living in contexts where the Christian church has a long and storied history, may have a difficult time reading the book of Acts in this way. He was suggesting that we in the West may find it hard to identify with the struggles and needs of the early disciples, and thus we do not read with the same sense of solidarity or with the same sense of urgency.

I believe that this conversation touches on perhaps the greatest contribution the Pentecostal movement is making to the larger church world: the Pentecostal movement is calling the church universal to take a fresh look at Luke's two-volume work. And in the process, it is encouraging the church to consider once again its own understanding and its own need of the Holy Spirit's power. It is precisely here, in Luke-Acts, where we find the central and distinctive message of the Pentecostal movement. From the earliest days of the modern Pentecostal revival, Pentecostals have proclaimed that all Christians may, and indeed should, experience a baptism in the Holy Spirit "distinct from and subsequent to the experience of new birth."[43] This understanding of Spirit baptism flows naturally from the conviction that the Spirit came upon the disciples at Pentecost (Acts 2), not as the source of new covenant existence but rather as the source of power for effective witness. This understanding of Spirit baptism has given the modern Pentecostal movement its identity, its unifying experience, and its missiological focus.

The rapid growth of Pentecostal churches around the world, particularly in the Two-Thirds World, makes it difficult

> **The rapid growth of Pentecostal churches around the world, particularly in the Two-Thirds World, makes it difficult for churches in the West to ignore this movement and its theology.**

---

43   *Minutes of the 44th Session of the General Council of the Assemblies of God* (Portland, OR; August 6–11, 1991), 129.

for churches in the West to ignore this movement and its theology. Indeed, Pentecostal churches around the world have been growing with such rapidity that "some historians refer to the 20th century as the 'Pentecostal Century.'"[44] So, today, let us heed the call and turn once again to the pages of Luke-Acts. More specifically, let us examine Luke's understanding of Spirit baptism and its significance for Pentecostal theology. We will begin by looking at the manner in which the Reformed tradition has understood this New Testament metaphor, baptism in the Spirit. We shall then trace the distinctive manner in which Luke uses this term. Finally, we shall draw out the implications of our study for the contemporary church.

1. RETHINKING PAST ASSUMPTIONS

The Pentecostal understanding of Spirit baptism as an empowering for service distinct from conversion has not been accepted by many from various traditions within the Christian church, including the majority of Reformed scholars. John Calvin does not treat Spirit baptism in an intentional or focused way. However, when he does refer to baptism in the Spirit, he associates it with the regenerating work of the Spirit. Calvin declares, "'he baptizes us in the Holy Spirit and fire (Luke 3:16)'" so that we are brought into "the light of faith in his gospel . . . so regenerating us that we become new creatures."[45] Elsewhere Calvin speaks of the Holy Spirit as the "secret energy of the Spirit,

---

44   Vinson Synan, *The Century of the Holy Spirit: 100 Years of Pentecostal and Charismatic Renewal* (Nashville, TN: Thomas Nelson, 2001), 2.

45   Calvin, *Institutes*, 3.1.4 (I, 542). See also *Institutes*, 4.16.25 (II, 1348). All references to Calvin's Institutes are from John Calvin, *Institutes of the Christian Religion*, 2 vols., trans. F. L. Battles and ed. J. T. McNeill, Library of Christian Classics 20 (Philadelphia: Westminster Press, 1960).

by which we come to enjoy Christ and all his benefits."[46] He also describes the Spirit as "the bond by which Christ effectually unites us to himself."[47] In the context of Calvin's writing and thought, it would appear that this redemptive work of the Spirit is inaugurated with Spirit baptism.

Calvin does not give much attention to the empowering dimension of the Spirit's work. Although Calvin speaks frequently of the Holy Spirit as the "inward teacher,"[48] the power that illuminates the mind and opens the heart of the one who *hears* the gospel, he does not highlight the Spirit's role in empowering the one who *proclaims* the message. Perhaps this is partly due to his emphasis on the Spirit as making the sacraments effectual on the one hand and to his polemic against confirmation as a sacrament on the other. Calvin strongly objected to the notion that confirmation, a rite subsequent to water baptism, was a true sacrament. Some asserted that while the Spirit was conferred in water baptism for regeneration, in confirmation the Spirit was granted in order to equip the believer "for battle." Calvin, arguing that this practice lacked biblical support, concludes: "We see the oil—the gross and greasy liquid—nothing else."[49]

It is interesting to note that in the context of his rebuttal of confirmation, Calvin discusses the bestowal of the Spirit on previously baptized believers recorded in Acts 8:16. He states that Luke here does not deny that "they who believe in Christ with their hearts and confess him with their mouth are endowed with any gift of the Spirit (Romans 10:10)," rather Luke has "in mind the receiving of the Spirit, by which manifest powers

---

46   Calvin, *Institutes*, 3.1.1 (I, 537).

47   Ibid., 538.

48   Calvin, *Institutes*, 4.14.9 (II, 1284). See also *Institutes*, 3.1.4 (I, 541).

49   Calvin, *Institutes*, 4.19.5 (II, 1453).

and visible graces were received."[50] Calvin maintains, however, "those miraculous powers and manifest workings, which were dispensed by the laying on of hands, have ceased; and they have rightly lasted only for a time."[51]

Other scholars in the Reformed tradition may place the accent in slightly different places. Karl Barth, for example, separates more clearly Spirit baptism from water baptism.[52] Nevertheless most of the scholars in the Reformed tradition define Spirit baptism in essentially the same manner: God's miraculous transformation of the believer. Of the prominent Reformed scholars, Hendrikus Berkhof comes the closest to acknowledging a positive contribution on the part of Pentecostals. He views Spirit baptism in terms of regeneration, but he sees this consisting of three elements: justification, sanctification, and calling or vocation.[53] Berkhof credits Pentecostals with highlighting the vocational dimension of Spirit baptism and faults Calvin for largely ignoring it. But Berkhof also chides Pentecostals for defining Spirit baptism solely in vocational terms.

The common thread that ties together the perspectives of these Reformed theologians is the assumption that the New Testament presents a relatively unified picture concerning the work of the Spirit in general and baptism in the Spirit in particular. In 1 Corinthians 12:13 Paul clearly speaks of Spirit baptism as the means by which one is initiated into the body of Christ: "For we were

---

50   Calvin, *Institutes*, 4.19.8 (II, 1456).

51   Calvin, *Institutes*, 4.19.6 (II, 1454).

52   See Frank D. Macchia. "Astonished by Faithfulness to God: A Reflection on Karl Barth's Understanding of Spirit Baptism" in *The Spirit and Spirituality: Essays in Honour of Russell P. Spittler,* eds. W. Ma and R. Menzies (London: T & T Clark International, 2004), 164–776. I am indebted to Frank Macchia for his helpful comments on Barth and H. Berkhof.

53   Hendrikus Berkhof, *The Doctrine of the Holy Spirit* (Louisville: Westminster/John Knox, 1986), 46–56.

all baptized by one Spirit into one body—whether Jews or Greeks, slave or free—and we were all given the one Spirit to drink." And Paul, writing from an early stage in the life of the church, offers a rich and full account of the Spirit's work. Paul speaks of the Spirit as the source of cleansing (1 Cor. 6:11; Rom. 15:16), righteousness (Gal. 5:5; Rom. 8:1–17; Gal. 5:16–26), intimate fellowship with God (Gal. 4:6; Rom. 8:14–17), and knowledge of God (1 Cor. 2:6–16; 2 Cor. 3:3–18). He even describes that ultimate transformation, the resurrection, as a work of the Spirit (Rom. 8:11; 1 Cor. 15:42–49; Gal. 6:8). All of this suggests that from the very earliest days, the early church had a unified and highly developed pneumatology. Paul, Luke, and John speak with one voice: the Spirit is the very source of Christian existence. How, then, could Spirit baptism be anything less than the miraculous transformation of the believer?

Yet there are good reasons to question this reading of the New Testament data and the theological conclusions based upon it. I have argued elsewhere that a thorough study of Luke-Acts and the Pauline literature reveals that there was a process of development in the early church's understanding of the Spirit's work.[54] This, of course, is not a novel thesis and many scholars, from Hermann Gunkel to Gonzalo Haya-Prats, have reached similar conclusions.[55] My own study of the evidence, particularly

---

54   Robert P. Menzies, *The Development of Early Christian Pneumatology with Special Reference to Luke-Acts* (Sheffield: JSPT Press, 1991). I also argue that John's Gospel supports my development thesis. See Robert P. Menzies, "John's Place in the Development of Early Christian Pneumatology" in *The Spirit and Spirituality*, 41–52.

55   Hermann Gunkel, *The Influence of the Holy Spirit: The Popular View of the Apostolic Age and the Teaching of the Apostle Paul*, trans. R. A. Harrisville and P.A. Quanbeck II (Philadelphia: Fortress Press, 1979; German Original, 1888); Gonzalo Haya-Prats, *Empowered Believers: The Holy Spirit in the Book of Acts*, trans. Paul Elbert and Scott A. Ellington (Eugene, OR: Cascade Books, 2010); see also the sources cited in Menzies, *Development*, 18–28.

in Luke-Acts,[56] led me to conclude that Paul was the first Christian to attribute soteriological functions to the Spirit and that his distinctive insights did not impact the non-Pauline sectors of the early church until after the writing of Luke-Acts (approximately 70 AD). The key point for our study is the affirmation that Luke's theology of the Spirit is *different* from that of Paul. Unlike Paul, who frequently speaks of the soteriological dimension of the Spirit's work, Luke consistently portrays the Spirit as a charismatic or, more precisely, a prophetic gift, the source of power for service.

A theology of the Spirit that is truly biblical must do justice to the pneumatology of *each* biblical author.

The important implications of this conclusion cannot be missed. If this is indeed the case, then the charismatic dimension of the Spirit to which Luke bears witness must be placed alongside the soteriological dimension so prominent in the writings of Paul. Certainly a theology of the Spirit that is truly biblical must do justice to the pneumatology of *each* biblical author.

Additionally, by placing the Pentecost account within the framework of Luke's distinctive theology of the Spirit, we can argue with considerable force that the Spirit came upon the disciples at Pentecost, not as the source of new covenant existence but, rather, as the source of power for effective witness—which, incidentally, is exactly what Luke states in Acts 1:8. Since this Pentecostal gift, this baptism in the Spirit, is charismatic rather than soteriological in character, it must be distinguished

---

56   See Robert P. Menzies, *Development* and the slightly revised version, *Empowered for Witness: The Spirit in Luke-Acts* (Sheffield: Sheffield Academic Press, 1994). See also Menzies and Menzies, *Spirit and Power*.

from the gift of the Spirit—and even the baptism in the Spirit in 1 Corinthians 12:13—that Paul so clearly associates with conversion and regeneration. Here, then, is a strong argument for the Pentecostal understanding of baptism in the Spirit—that is, that Spirit baptism in the Lukan sense is logically distinct from conversion. This distinction and uniquely missiological purpose is a reflection of Luke's distinctive theology of the Spirit.

This recognition that Luke's theology of the Spirit is *different* from that of Paul is then crucial for a Pentecostal understanding of Spirit baptism. As we

> **Luke consistently portrays the gift of the Spirit as a prophetic enabling.**

have seen, some Reformed theologians would agree that Luke emphasizes the Spirit's role in equipping the church for its mission. Berkhof speaks of the "vocational" dimension of the Spirit's work. Calvin refers to the bestowal of "manifest powers" and "visible graces." But at the same time, they still maintain that Luke, in a manner similar to Paul, relates Spirit baptism to salvation. This vocational or charismatic dimension of baptism in the Spirit is merely a reflection of Luke's *emphasis*. In this way, Reformed theologians can speak of the gift of the Spirit received at Pentecost as the essential element of conversion, the means whereby the disciples experience the blessings of the new covenant (i.e., cleansing, justification, moral transformation), even though they might also acknowledge that divine enabling is prominent in Luke's narrative. But, if our summary of Luke's pneumatology above is correct, this will not do. As we have stated, Luke views the gift of the Spirit *exclusively* in charismatic terms. His narrative reflects more than a special *emphasis*; it bears witness to a *distinctive theology* of the Spirit. Consequently, the charismatic character of Luke's baptism in the Spirit cannot be questioned, and Luke's unique and Pentecostal contribution to biblical pneumatology must be given its due.

As I have stated, the evidence suggests that Luke's theology of the Spirit is indeed *different* from that of Paul—ultimately complementary, but different. Luke not only fails to refer to soteriological aspects of the Spirit's work, his narrative presupposes a pneumatology that does not include this dimension (e.g., Luke 11:13; Acts 8:4–25; 18:24–19:7).[57] Of course a detailed examination of Luke's two-volume work is required to defend this assertion. I have provided this elsewhere.[58] In this brief chapter, however, I believe I can make my point by focusing on three key passages associated with the term baptism in the Holy Spirit: John the Baptist's prophecy (Luke 3:16–17); Jesus' sermon at Nazareth (Luke 4:17–19); and references to the promise of the Spirit (Luke 24:49; Acts 1:4, 2:33, 2:39).

2. LUKE'S DISTINCTIVE PERSPECTIVE

Throughout his two-volume work, Luke consistently portrays the gift of the Spirit as a prophetic enabling. Whether it is John in his mother's womb, Jesus at the Jordan, or the disciples at Pentecost, the Spirit comes upon them all as the source of prophetic inspiration, granting special insight and inspiring speech. This should not surprise us, since the literature of intertestamental Judaism also identifies the Spirit with prophetic inspiration.[59]

---

57 I have also observed that the traditions of the primitive church utilized by Paul fail to attribute soteriological functions to the Spirit. See Menzies, *Development*, 282–315.

58 Menzies, *Development* and *Empowered for Witness*.

59 This is the dominant perspective. The only exceptions are found in sapiential writings and are exceedingly rare.

This pneumatological perspective shapes the key Lukan texts that speak of baptism in the Holy Spirit. To these texts we now turn.

John the Baptist's Prophecy

John the Baptist's prophecy concerning the One who will baptize in Spirit and fire, recorded in Luke 3:16–17, is particularly important for our study:

> John answered them all, "I baptize you with water. But one more powerful than I will come, the thongs of whose sandals I am not worthy to untie. He will baptize you with the Holy Spirit and fire. His winnowing fork is in his hand to clear his threshing floor and to gather the wheat into his barn, but he will burn up the chaff with unquenchable fire." (Luke 3:16–17)

The interpretation of this prophecy—specifically, the functions it attributes to the Spirit—is crucial, for Luke clearly sees this prophecy at least partially fulfilled at Pentecost in the disciples' baptism in the Spirit (Acts 1:4–5). James Dunn speaks for many when he states that the prophecy presents that Spirit as "purgative and refining for those who had repented, destructive ... for those who remained impenitent."[60] However, I believe this interpretation must be rejected in light of the Jewish background, the immediate context with its winnowing metaphor, and the larger context of Luke-Acts.

The Jewish background is particularly instructive. There are no pre-Christian references to a messianic bestowal of the Spirit

---

60   James Dunn, *Baptism in the Holy Spirit* (London: SCM Press, 1970), 13.

CHAPTER TWO: BAPTISM IN THE HOLY SPIRIT

that purifies and transforms *the individual.* However, there are a wealth of passages that describe the Messiah as charismatically endowed with the Spirit of God so that He may rule and judge (e.g., *1 En.* 49:3; 62:2).[61] Isaiah 4:4 refers to the Spirit of God as the means by which the nation of Israel (not individuals!) shall be sifted with the righteous being separated from the wicked and the nation thus cleansed. Several texts tie these two concepts together. Perhaps most striking is Psalms of Solomon 17:26–37, a passage which describes how the Messiah, "powerful in the Holy Spirit" (17:37), shall purify Israel by ejecting all aliens and sinners from the nation. Isaiah 11:2–4 declares that the Spirit-empowered Messiah will slay the wicked "with the breath [*ruach*] of his lips."[62] Against this background it is not difficult to envision the Spirit of God as an instrument employed by the Messiah to sift and cleanse the nation. Indeed, these texts suggest that when John referred in metaphorical language to the messianic deluge of the Spirit, he had in mind Spirit-inspired oracles of judgment uttered by the Messiah (cf. Isa. 11:4), blasts of the Spirit that would separate the wheat from the chaff.

Luke, writing in light of Pentecost, sees the fuller picture and applies the prophecy to the Spirit-inspired witness of the early church (Acts 1:4–5). Through their witness, the wheat is separated from the chaff (Luke 3:17). This interpretation is reinforced by the winnowing metaphor, which portrays the wind as the source of sifting. Since the term translated "wind" in Greek (*pneuma*) and Hebrew (*ruach*) is also used to refer to "the Spirit," the symbolism is particularly striking. This Spirit-inspired

---

61   Although works such as *1 Enoch, Psalms of Solomon,* and various writings from Qumran stand outside the Protestant canon of Scripture, they do shed valuable light on the theological perspective of first-century Jews. For this reason, I cite them here.

62   This passage is echoed in *1 Enoch* 62:2 and 1QSb 5:24–25.

witness and its impact is foreshadowed by Simeon's prophecy in Luke 2:34. Simeon, with reference to Jesus, declares: "This child is destined to cause the falling and rising of many in Israel."

In short, John described the Spirit's work, not as cleansing repentant individuals but, rather, as a blast of the "breath" of God that would sift the nation. Luke sees this prophecy, at least with reference to the sifting work of the Spirit, fulfilled in the Spirit-inspired mission of the church. The essential point for our purpose is that Luke presents the Spirit here, not as the source of cleansing for the individual but as the animating force behind the church's witness.

Jesus and the Spirit

Luke declares that the coming Spirit-baptizer was Himself anointed with the Spirit (Luke 3:22; 4:18; Acts 10:38). This leads us to another question of central importance: what significance does Luke attach to Jesus' pneumatic anointing? How does Luke understand and present this important event?

The description of Jesus' pneumatic anointing accounts for only two sentences in Luke's Gospel (Luke 3:21–22). Fortunately, Luke has provided an extended commentary on the significance of this event. This commentary is found in Luke's account of Jesus' sermon at Nazareth. This account is recorded in Luke 4:16–30, but I shall only quote the portion critical for our task, vv. 17–19:

> The scroll of the prophet Isaiah was handed to him. Unrolling it, he found the place where it is written:
> "The Spirit of the LORD is on me,
> because he has anointed me to preach good news to the poor.

He has sent me to proclaim freedom for the prisoners
and recovery of sight for the blind,
to release the oppressed,
to proclaim the year of the LORD's favor."
(Luke 4:17–19)

The significance of this passage is underscored by a comparison with Mark's Gospel. Luke normally follows Mark's chronology of Jesus' ministry very closely. But here, Luke takes an event—Jesus' ministry in Nazareth—that occurs in the middle of Mark's Gospel (Mk. 6:1–6) and places it at the forefront of his description of Jesus' ministry. Of course Luke's account of the Nazareth event is much fuller than Mark's and includes details important for Luke's purposes. That these purposes include helping the reader understand the significance of Jesus' reception of the Spirit is confirmed, not only by the content of the quotation from Isaiah 61:1–2, which we have just read (Luke 4:17–19), but also by the references to the Spirit in Luke's narrative that link the accounts of Jesus' anointing (Luke 3:21–22) with his sermon at Nazareth (Luke 4:16–30). Luke reminds us in Luke 4:1 that Jesus was "full of the Holy Spirit" as He entered into the desert of temptation. And he also affirms that Jesus departed this desert experience "in the power of the Spirit" (Luke 4:14). With this "redactional bridge," Luke highlights the connection between Jesus' pneumatic anointing and His sermon at Nazareth. So, the sermon at Nazareth is important because it calls us *to look back*—to look back and understand more fully the significance of Jesus' reception of the Spirit.

However, this passage also calls us *to look forward.* Luke crafts his narrative so that the parallels between Jesus' experience of the Spirit (Luke 3–4) and that of the disciples on the day of Pentecost (Acts 1–2) cannot be missed. Both accounts:

1. Are placed at the outset of Luke's Gospel on the one hand, and the book of Acts on the other
2. Associate the reception of the Spirit with prayer
3. Record visible and audible manifestations
4. Offer explanations of the event in the form of a sermon that alludes to the fulfillment of Old Testament prophecy

In this way, Luke presents Jesus' reception of the Spirit as a model for that of the disciples in Acts and future generations of believers, including his own (see Luke 11:13 and Acts 2:17).

It is evident, then, that this passage is crucial for understanding the significance of Jesus' reception of the Spirit and that of the disciples in Acts. It thus also provides important definition for Luke's understanding of Spirit baptism. With this in mind, let us address the question at hand: What significance does Luke attach to Jesus' pneumatic anointing? Luke's answer is unequivocal. The quotation from Isaiah, which plays such a prominent role in the narrative, answers our question with precision: Jesus' reception of the Spirit at the Jordan was the means by which He was equipped to carry out His messianic mission. Furthermore, the verbs in the text—"he has anointed me *to preach* good news to the poor. . . . He has sent me *to proclaim* freedom for the prisoners . . . *to proclaim* the year of the Lord's favor"—highlight *proclamation*, inspired speech, as the primary product of Jesus' anointing. In short, Luke presents Jesus' reception of the Spirit at the Jordan as a prophetic anointing, the means by which He was equipped to carry out His divinely appointed task.

The Promise of the Father

Luke refers to "the promise" of the Spirit four times in close proximity (Luke 24:49; Acts 1:4; 2:33, 39). "The promise" is identified with the Pentecostal gift of the Spirit (2:33) and explicitly defined: reception of "the promise" will result in the disciples being "clothed with power from on high" and enable them to be effective "witnesses" (Luke 24:48–49; Acts 1:8). Furthermore, for Luke "the promise" with reference to the Spirit refers to the gift of the Spirit of prophecy promised in Joel 2:28–32. This is made clear through Luke's citation of Joel 2:28–32 in Acts 2:17–21, and further emphasized in his redactional introduction of the citation.

Luke presents Jesus' reception of the Spirit as a model for that of the disciples in Acts and future generations of believers, including his own.

This introduction includes the phrase "God says" (Acts 2:17) and thus identifies the prophecy of Joel as "the promise of the Father"—the full description of "the promise" in three of the four Lukan references (Luke 24:49; Acts 1:4; 2:33). In Joel's prophecy the Spirit comes as the source of prophetic inspiration, a point that Luke highlights by inserting the phrase "and they will prophesy" (Acts 2:18) into the Greek text of Joel. Another alteration, Luke's transformation of Joel's "slaves" into "servants of God"—accomplished by his double insertion of "my" into Acts 2:18—highlights what is implicit in the Joel text:

the gift of the Spirit is given only to those who are members of the community of salvation. Thus Luke's explicit definitions (Luke 24:49; Acts 1:4–8) and his use of the Joel citation indicate that the "promise" of the Spirit, initially fulfilled at Pentecost (Acts 2:4), enables the disciples to take up their prophetic vocation to the world.

Although the Lukan "promise" of the Spirit must be interpreted in light of Joel's promise concerning the restoration of the Spirit of prophecy, Acts 2:39 does include an additional element. The passage reads:

> Peter replied, "Repent and be baptized, every one of you, in the name of Jesus Christ so that your sins may be forgiven. And you will receive the gift of the Holy Spirit. The promise is for you and your children and for all who are far off—for all whom the LORD our God will call. (Acts 2:38–39).

In Acts 2:39, Luke extends the range of the promise envisioned to include the promise of salvation offered in Joel 2:32 (as well as the promise of the Spirit of prophecy in Joel 2:28). Acts 2:39 echoes the language of Joel 2:32/Acts 2:21: "everyone who calls on the name of the LORD will be saved." In Acts 2:39, Luke extends the range of "the promise" to include this salvific dimension because the audience addressed now includes non-believers.

Yet we must not miss the fact that "the promise" of Acts 2:39 embraces more than the experience of conversion. Consistent with the other references to "the promise" (Luke 24:49; Acts 1:4; 2:33), the promised gift of the Spirit in Acts 2:39 refers to the promise of Joel 2:28, and thus it is a promise of prophetic enabling granted to the repentant. The promise of Acts 2:39, like the promise of

Jesus in Acts 1:8, points beyond the restoration of the faithful of Israel: salvation is offered (Joel 2:32), but the promise includes the renewal of Israel's prophetic vocation to be a light to the nations (Joel 2:28; cf. Isaiah 49:6 and Acts 1:8).

Some have criticized this approach, suggesting that we should read Luke's earlier references to the promise of the Spirit in light of the promise of salvation offered in Acts 2:39.[63] Yet, as we have seen, Acts 2:39 does not indicate that the Spirit comes as the source of new covenant existence. Rather, it simply reminds us that the prophecy of Joel 2:28–32 includes two elements: the gift of the Spirit of prophecy (v. 28) and the offer of salvation to those who call upon the name of the Lord (v. 32). Acts 2:39 refers to both, but does not suggest the two are identical. Indeed, this sort of equation runs counter to Luke's explicit statements in Luke 24:49 and Acts 1:4–8, his use and redaction of the Joel citation in Acts 2:17–18, and the broader context of his two-volume work. In particular, Luke's description of baptized believers (Acts 8:16) and disciples (Acts 19:2), all without the Spirit, raises insurmountable problems for this position.

Of course it is possible to argue that Luke's understanding of the promise of the Spirit—clearly shaped by Joel 2:28–32—was also informed by a number of other Old Testament prophecies regarding the Spirit's eschatological role, especially Isaiah 44:3–5 and Ezekiel 36:26–27. Yet this approach fails to examine how these Old Testament texts were interpreted in the Judaism that gave rise to the Christianity Luke knew. We see, for example, that the transformation of the heart referred to in Ezekiel 36:26–27 was viewed as a *prerequisite* for the eschatological bestowal of the Spirit and that the rabbis interpreted Isaiah 44:3 as a

---

63   James D. G. Dunn, "Baptism in the Spirit: A Response to Pentecostal Scholarship," *Journal of Pentecostal Theology* 3 (1993): 12, 21.

reference to the outpouring of the Spirit of prophecy on Israel. Rather than simply reading our own agenda and exegesis into the first-century setting, surely it is better to ask how those Jews closest in time to the early Christians understood the relevant texts and what significance they attached to them.

This is particularly important at this point, for the eschatological outpouring of the Spirit was generally interpreted in light of Joel 2:28–29 as a restoration of the Spirit of prophecy. By way of contrast, Ezekiel 36:26–27 was usually interpreted as a prophecy concerning the end-time removal of the evil "impulse," and most frequently without reference to the activity of the Spirit. Indeed, the eradication of the evil "impulse" was presented as a prerequisite for the end-time bestowal of the Spirit of prophecy.[64] This means that calls for us to interpret the promise of the Spirit in light of a plethora of Old Testament texts conflict with the evidence from early Jewish sources and Luke's own hand. Luke, unlike Paul and John, cites none of these other Old Testament texts. There simply is no evidence to support the notion that by referring to Joel 2:28–32, Luke intended his readers to think of some commonly expected, all-embracing soteriological bestowal of the Spirit.

Should the collocation of repentance, baptism, and reception of the Spirit in Acts 2:38 cause us to reconsider these conclusions? I think not, for it tells us little about the nature of the gift of the Spirit. While the collocation may indicate that for Luke the rite of water baptism is normally accompanied by the bestowal of the Spirit, Luke's usage elsewhere suggests that even this conclusion may be overstating the case. There is certainly nothing in the text that would suggest that the Spirit

---

64   For further discussion of these points and the relevant Jewish texts see Menzies, *Development*, 52–112, especially 104–11.

is presented here as the source of new covenant existence. If it could be established that the text presupposes an inextricable bond between water baptism and forgiveness of sins on the one hand and reception of the Spirit on the other, then we would need to reconsider our position. However, this conclusion is clearly unwarranted. Since Luke fails to develop a strong link between water baptism and the bestowal of the Spirit elsewhere, and regularly separates the rite from the gift (Luke 3:21–22; Acts 8:12–17; 9:17–18; 10:44; and 18:24–25), the phrase "and you will receive the gift of the Holy Spirit" in Acts 2:38 should be interpreted as a promise that the Spirit shall be "imparted to those who are already converted and baptized."[65] In any case, the most that can be gleaned from the text is that repentance and water baptism are the normal prerequisites for reception of the Spirit, which is promised to every believer.

> **Repentance and water baptism are the normal prerequisites for reception of the Spirit, which is promised to every believer.**

In short, I believe it is prudent to interpret Acts 2:38–39 in the light of Luke's explicit testimony concerning the promise of the Spirit recorded in Luke 24:49, Acts 1:4, and Acts 2:17–18—all of which describe the pneumatic gift as a prophetic enabling for the missionary task. This reading also fits nicely with Luke's usage elsewhere, especially his otherwise problematic description of baptized believers who have not received the Holy Spirit (Acts 8:4–17; cf. 18:24–19:7). Additionally, calls for us to interpret the promise of the Spirit against the backdrop of a plethora of Old

---

65   E. Schweizer, "πνεῦμα," in *Theological Dictionary of the New Testament*, vol. 6, eds. Gerhard Freidrich and Gerhard Kittel (Grand Rapids: Eerdmans, 1980), 412.

Testament texts, none of which are mentioned by Luke or linked in the suggested manner with the Joel text by contemporary Jewish thinkers, must be rejected. Again, wisdom dictates that we understand the promise of the Spirit against the backdrop of the text that Luke does cite, Joel 2:28–32, and contemporary Jewish expectations.

Summary

I have argued that Luke interprets the sifting and separating activity of the Spirit of which John prophesied (Luke 3:16–17) to be accomplished in the Spirit-empowered mission of the church. Thus, for Luke, John's prophecy is initially fulfilled in the Pentecostal bestowal of the Spirit. At Pentecost, the disciples are baptized in the Holy Spirit and thereby enabled to bear bold witness for Jesus (Acts 1:8). In a broader sense, through the disciples' Spirit-inspired preaching, the entire nation is baptized in the Holy Spirit; for through their preaching about Jesus the people are sifted like the wind sifts the chaff from the grain (cf. Luke 2:34).

I have also asserted that the Spirit came upon Jesus at the Jordan in order to equip Him for His messianic task (Luke 3:22; 4:18–19). This is the unambiguous message of Jesus' dramatic sermon at Nazareth. The striking parallels between Jesus' pneumatic anointing at the Jordan and that of the disciples at Pentecost suggest that Luke interpreted the latter event in light of the former: Pentecost was for the disciples what the Jordan was for Jesus. The logical corollary is that at Pentecost the Spirit came upon the disciples in order to enable them to fulfill their divinely appointed task.

Finally, I have affirmed that for Luke the "promise" with reference to the Spirit (Luke 24:49; Acts 1:4; 2:33, 38–39) refers to the gift of the Spirit of prophecy promised by Joel. This "promise," initially fulfilled at Pentecost, enables the disciples to take up their prophetic vocation to the world (Acts 1:8). The message is repeated for emphasis—it comes at the end of his gospel (Luke 24:49) and at the beginning of his record of the mission of the early church (Acts 1:4)—to insure that we will not miss it.

Indeed, the message that emerges from each of these texts is unified and clear. According to Luke, the Spirit, understood to be the source of prophetic activity, came upon the disciples at Pentecost in order to equip them for their prophetic vocation (i.e., for their role as "witnesses"). This "baptism in the Holy Spirit" does not cleanse the disciples nor grant them a new ability to keep the law; rather, this "baptism in the Holy Spirit" drives them forward in the face of opposition and enables them to bear bold witness for Christ.

3. IMPLICATIONS FOR THE CHURCH TODAY

We are now able to draw out some of the implications for the contemporary church that arise from Luke's distinctive understanding of Spirit baptism. Let us begin by affirming what Pentecostals and the Reformed tradition hold in common.

We can all agree that Calvin and the other great Reformed theologians have read Paul well.[66] Calvin correctly highlights the role of the Spirit in regeneration, in making the sacraments effectual, in justification. The Holy Spirit is the great "inner

---

66   Of course, a key exception would be the cessationist perspective that many in the Reformed tradition tend to read into Paul's epistles.

teacher" who bears witness in our hearts to the truth of the gospel. So, together, we affirm that every Christian receives the life-giving and indwelling Spirit. There is no Christian without the Spirit; there is no Christian existence apart from the Spirit's work in our lives. Furthermore, we can also agree that in 1 Corinthians 12:13, Paul clearly refers to this salvific work of the Spirit as a baptism in the Holy Spirit.

However, Pentecostals raise another important question: What is Luke's contribution to this discussion? Or, to put it another way, what is Luke's understanding of baptism in the Holy Spirit? Pentecostals believe that there is more to be said on this matter than that which is contained in the Pauline epistles. We affirm that Luke has a unique and special contribution to make to a holistic biblical theology of the Spirit. We also believe that the clarity and vigor of Luke's contribution is lost when his narrative is read through Pauline lenses. Luke has a distinctive voice, and it is a voice the church needs to hear.

> **There is no Christian without the Spirit; there is no Christian existence apart from the Spirit's work in our lives.**

Luke's understanding of baptism in the Holy Spirit, I have argued, is different from that of Paul. It is missiological rather than soteriological in nature. The Spirit of Pentecost is, in reality, the Spirit for others—the Spirit that compels and empowers the church to bring the "good news" of Jesus to a lost and dying world. It is this Lukan, missiological perspective that shapes a Pentecostal understanding of baptism in the Holy Spirit. Of course, Pentecostals recognize that we must do justice to Paul's soteriological contribution by emphasizing the Spirit's role in conversion, regeneration, and sanctification. Yet Pentecostals feel justified in speaking of a baptism in the Spirit that is distinct from conversion, an anointing for service, for we see this as accurately reflecting Luke's terminology and theology.

Pentecostals, then, recognize that the New Testament speaks of two baptisms in the Spirit—one that is soteriological and initiates the believer into the body of Christ (1 Cor. 12:13) and one that is missiological and empowers the believer for service (Acts 1:8). However, Pentecostals feel that it is particularly appropriate to adopt Luke's language and speak of the Pentecostal gift as a "baptism in the Holy Spirit." After all, this baptism in the Holy Spirit is promised to every believer, to all of the servants of God (Acts 2:18). And Luke uses the phrase on three occasions, Paul only once. Pentecostals also fear that if Paul's language is employed and the gift of the Spirit received at conversion is designated "the baptism in the Holy Spirit," then a proper understanding of the Pentecostal gift will be lost.

The tendency in Protestant churches has been to read Luke in the light of Paul. Paul addresses pastoral concerns in the church; Luke writes a missionary manifesto. Perhaps this explains why Protestant discussions of the Spirit have centered more on his work in the Word and sacraments, the "inner witness" of the Spirit, and less on his mission to the world. As we have noted, Reformed theologians tend to associate the Pentecostal gift with conversion and regeneration, which effectively blunts the sharpness of Luke's message. When the Pentecostal gift of the Spirit is understood in soteriological terms, Luke's missiological focus and our expectation of it is lost. For it is always possible to argue, as many do, that while all experience the soteriological dimension of the Pentecostal gift at conversion, only a select few receive gifts of missiological power. Yet Luke calls us to remember that the church (every member, not just the clergy!), by virtue of its reception of the Pentecostal gift, is a prophetic community empowered for a missionary task.

CONCLUSION

I would like to conclude by noting one important link to the Pentecostal understanding of Spirit baptism within the Reformed tradition. It is found in the writings of the first great Reformed theologian, Ulrich Zwingli. In his *Commentary on True and False Religion,* Zwingli refers to two baptisms of the Holy Spirit. Zwingli writes:

> The baptism of the Holy Spirit, then, is twofold. First, there is the baptism by which all are flooded within who trust in Christ. . . . Second, there is the external baptism of the Holy Spirit, just as there is the baptism of water. Drenched with this, pious men began at once to speak in foreign tongues [Acts 2:4–11]. . . . This latter baptism of the Holy Spirit is not necessary, but the former is so very necessary that no one can be saved without it. . . . Now we are not all imbued with the sign of tongues, but all of us who are pious have been made faithful by the enlightenment and drawing of the Holy Spirit.[67]

Zwingli did not elaborate further on his understanding of two baptisms of the Spirit, but his perspective on Pentecost appears to be quite similar to what I have already outlined.

---

67   Ulrich Zwingli, *Commentary on True and False Religion,* eds. S. M. Jackson and C. N. Heller (Durham, NC: The Labyrinth Press, 1981), 187–88.

The Reformed tradition has made great contributions to the modern Pentecostal movement. Chief among them is its call to recognize the progressive nature of the sanctifying work of the Spirit in the life of the believer. Reformed theologians have correctly encouraged Pentecostals to acknowledge that power and purity are not necessarily linked. Reception of Pentecostal power is no guarantee of spiritual maturity. Regrettably, we Pentecostals often have been slow to acknowledge this truth. But this important legacy of the Reformed tradition is there, nonetheless. Perhaps by stimulating Reformed scholars to take a fresh look at Zwingli's and Luke's writings, the Pentecostal movement can pay back a bit of the enormous debt it owes.

CHAPTER THREE

THE ROLE OF TONGUES IN LUKE-ACTS

W e have noted that Pentecostals have a distinctive hermeneutic, a particular way of reading the Bible. We Pentecostals have always read the narrative of Acts, and particularly the account of the Pentecostal outpouring of the Holy Spirit (Acts 2), as a model for our own lives. The stories of Acts are our stories and we read them with a sense of eager expectation.

I am convinced that this simple hermeneutic, this straightforward approach to reading Acts as a model for the church today, is one of the key reasons why an emphasis on speaking in tongues played such an important role in the formation of the modern Pentecostal movement. Certainly the link between speaking in tongues and baptism in the Holy Spirit has marked the modern Pentecostal movement since its inception and without this linkage it is doubtful whether the movement would have seen the light of day, let alone survived.[68]

Glossolalia has been crucially important for Pentecostals the world over for many reasons, but I would suggest that two are of particular importance.[69] First, speaking in tongues highlights, embodies, and validates the unique way that Pentecostals read the book of Acts: Acts is not simply a historical document; rather, Acts presents a model for the life of the contemporary church. Thus, tongues serve as a sign that "their experience" is "our experience" and that all of the gifts of the Spirit (including the "sign gifts") are valid for the church today. Secondly, tongues calls the church to recognize and remember its true identity: the church is nothing less than a community of end-time prophets called and empowered to bear bold witness for Jesus. In short, the Pentecostal approach to tongues symbolizes significant aspects of the movement: its hermeneutic (Acts and the apostolic church represent a model for the church today) and its theological center (the prophetic and missionary nature of the Pentecostal gift). For Pentecostals, then, tongues serve as a sign that the calling and power of the apostolic church are valid for contemporary believers.

> **For Pentecostals . . . tongues serve as a sign that the calling and power of the apostolic church are valid for contemporary believers.**

---

68   Synan, "The Role of Tongues," 67–82.

69   The notion that the doctrine of initial evidence is only important to North American Pentecostals is spurious. This chapter is an edited version of a paper that I presented in Mandarin Chinese to a group of Assemblies of God ministers in Taiwan. They asked me to present a paper on initial evidence and this is the result. I could give many other illustrations of a keen interest in and commitment to speaking in tongues and the "initial evidence" doctrine from the Philippines, Singapore, Malaysia, and China.

In this chapter I would like to explore, from Luke's perspective, the role of tongues in the life of the church and the individual believer. I will first highlight the importance of starting our inquiry with the right mindset by describing the assumptions regarding tongues that should inform our study. I will then attempt to elucidate Luke's perspective on tongues, particularly his attitude toward the role of tongues in his church. Following this, I shall seek to describe Luke's understanding of the role of tongues in the life of the individual believer. Finally, I shall summarize my findings and their significance for contemporary Christians.

1. IMPORTANT ASSUMPTIONS: TONGUES OR LANGUAGES?

Many Christians seeking to examine the biblical teaching on tongues begin with faulty assumptions. Chief among these would be the notion that glossolalia was either non-existent in the early church or, at the most, that it was experienced very rarely by a limited few. The teaching, prevalent in some quarters, that references to "speaking in tongues" in the New Testament typically denote the supernatural ability to preach in a foreign language previously unknown to the speaker (xenolalia), has cast a long shadow. Furthermore, the impression is often given that the New Testament authors rarely discuss this strange practice and that, when they do, they do so with great hesitation and are largely negative and condescending in their remarks. However, a review of the biblical evidence, as we shall see, suggests that these assumptions are flawed and need to be reconsidered.

The phenomenon of speaking in tongues is actually described in numerous passages in the New Testament.[70] In 1 Corinthians 12–14 Paul refers to the gift of tongues (γλώσσαις)[71] and uses the phrase λαλέω γλώσσαις to designate unintelligible utterances inspired by the Spirit.[72] The fact that this gift of tongues refers to unintelligible utterances (e.g., the glossolalia experienced in contemporary Pentecostal churches) rather than known human languages is confirmed by the fact that Paul explicitly states that these tongues must be interpreted if they are to be understood (1 Cor. 14:6–19, 28; cf. 12:10, 30).

In Acts 10:46 and 19:6 Luke also uses the phrase λαλέω γλώσσαις to designate utterances inspired by the Spirit. In Acts 10:46 Peter and his colleagues hear Cornelius and his household "speaking in tongues and praising God." Acts 19:6 states that the Ephesian disciples "spoke in tongues and prophesied." The literary parallels between the descriptions of speaking in tongues in these passages and 1 Corinthians 12–14 are impressive. All of these texts: (1) associate speaking in tongues with the inspiration of the Holy Spirit; (2) utilize similar vocabulary (λαλέω γλώσσαις); and (3) describe inspired speech associated with worship and prophetic pronouncements. Additionally, since 1 Corinthians 12–14 clearly speaks of unintelligible utterances and there is no indication in either of the Acts passages that known languages are being spoken—indeed, there is no apparent need for a miracle of xenolalia in either instance (what foreign language would they have spoken?)—most English translations (including the NRSV) translate the occurrences of λαλέω γλώσσαις in these texts with reference to speaking in tongues.

---

70   See 1 Cor. 12–14; Acts 2:4; 10:46; 19:6; note also Mark 16:17 and Romans 8:26–27.

71   1 Cor. 12:10; 12:28; 13:8; 14:22, 26.

72   1 Cor. 12:30; 13:1; 14:2, 4, 6, 13, 18, 23, 27, 39.

The references to γλώσσαις in Acts 2:1–13, however, raise interesting questions for those seeking to understand this passage. The first occurrence of γλώσσαις is found in Acts 2:3, where it refers to the visionary "tongues of fire" that appear and then separate and rest on each of the disciples present. Then, in Acts 2:4 we read that those present were all filled with the Holy Spirit and began to "speak in other tongues (λαλεῖν ἑτέραις γλώσσαις) as the Spirit enabled them." This phenomenon creates confusion among the Jews of the crowd who, we are told, represent "every nation under heaven" (Acts 2:5). The crowd gathered in astonishment because "each one heard them speaking in his own language" (διαλέκτῳ; Acts 2:6). These details are repeated as Luke narrates the response of the astonished group: "Are not all these men who are speaking Galileans? Then how is it that each of us hears them in his own native language (διαλέκτῳ; Acts 2:7–8)?" After the crowd lists in amazement the various nations represented by those present, they declare, "we hear them declaring the wonders of God in our own tongues (γλώσσαις ; Acts 2:11)!"

> **The disciples are enabled by the Spirit to declare "the wonders of God" in human languages that they had not previously learned.**

Since Acts 2:11 clearly relates γλώσσαις to the various human languages of those present in the crowd, most scholars interpret the "tongues" (γλώσσαις) of Acts 2:4 and 2:11 as referring to intelligible speech. The disciples are enabled by the Spirit to declare "the wonders of God" in human languages that they had not previously learned. This reading of the text has encouraged the NRSV to translate γλώσσαις in Acts 2:4 and 2:11 with the term "language."

However, it should be noted that this text has been interpreted differently. Some scholars, admittedly a minority, have argued that the "tongues" (γλώσσαις) of Acts 2:4 refer to unintelligible utterances inspired by the Spirit.[73] According to this reading, the miracle that occurs at Pentecost is two-fold: first, the disciples are inspired by the Holy Spirit to declare the "wonders of God" in a spiritual language that is unintelligible to human beings (i.e., glossolalia); secondly, the Jews in the crowd who represent a diverse group of countries are miraculously enabled to understand the glossolalia of the disciples so that it appears to them that the disciples are speaking in each of their own mother-tongues. Although this position may at first sight appear to be special pleading, as Jenny Everts points out, there are in fact a number of reasons to take it seriously.[74]

First, it should be noted that Luke uses two different terms, both of which can refer to language, in Acts 2:1–13: γλώσσαις (Acts 2:4, 11) and διάλεκτος (Acts 2:6, 8). The term διάλεκτος clearly refers to intelligible speech in Acts 2:6, 8 and it may well be that Luke is consciously contrasting this term with "the more obscure expression of ἑτέραις γλώσσαις" in Acts 2:4.[75] Given the usage of the term, γλώσσαις, elsewhere in the New Testament, particularly when it is associated with the coming of the Holy Spirit, this suggestion is entirely plausible. Luke certainly had other options before him: he could have referred to languages

---

73   See Everts, "Tongues or Languages? Contextual Consistency in the Translation of Acts 2," *Journal of Pentecostal Theology* 4 (1994), 74, n. 9 and the works she cites, the most recent being J. L. Sherrill, *They Speak with Other Tongues* (New York: McGraw-Hill, 1964), 105–106.

74   Everts, "Tongues," 74–75. I am largely dependent on Everts for the points that follow.

75   Ibid, 75.

in other ways, as the usage of διάλεκτος in Acts 2:6–8 indicates. However, in Acts 2:4 he chooses to use the term γλώσσαις, which reappears in similar contexts in Acts 10:46 and 19:6.

Second, it may well be that the phrase τῇ ἰδίᾳ διαλέκτῳ ("in his own language") modifies the verbs of hearing in Acts 2:6 and in Acts 2:8. This is certainly the case in Acts 2:8: "How is it that each of us hears them in his own native language?" Everts notes that, if we read Acts 2:6 in a similar way, "these two verses would imply that each individual heard the entire group of disciples speaking the individual's native language."[76] All of this indicates that Luke may not be using γλώσσαις (Acts 2:4, 11) and διάλεκτος (Acts 2:6, 8) simply as synonyms.

Third, the major objection to this interpretation is the fact that in Acts 2:11 γλώσσαις is used as a synonym for διάλεκτος: "we hear them declaring the wonders of God in our own tongues" (γλώσσαις). However, it should be noticed that in Acts 2:1–13 Luke may be intentionally playing on the multiple meanings of γλῶσσα (tongue). In Acts 2:3 the term refers to the shape of a tongue ("tongues of fire"). In Acts 2:11 it refers to a person's mother-tongue or native language. Given the term's usage elsewhere in the New Testament, is it not likely that Luke intended his readers to understand his use of the term in Acts 2:4 as a reference to unintelligible speech inspired by the Holy Spirit (glossolalia)?

Fourth, this reading of the text offers a coherent reason for the reaction of the bystanders who thought that the disciples were drunk. While it is hard to imagine the crowd reacting this way if the disciples are simply speaking in foreign languages, the crowd's reaction is entirely understandable if the disciples are speaking in tongues (glossolalia).

---

76   Ibid.

In short, the evidence suggests that Luke's references to speaking in tongues (λαλέω γλώσσαις) in Acts 10:46, 19:6, and quite possibly (but less certain) 2:4, designate unintelligible utterances inspired by the Spirit rather than the speaking of human languages previously not learned. The crucial point to note here is that in Acts 2:4 γλώσσαις may mean something quite different from what is suggested by the translation, "languages." The translation "tongues," on the other hand, with its broader range of meaning, not only captures well the nuances of both possible interpretations noted above, it also retains the verbal connection Luke intended between Acts 2:4, Acts 10:46, and Acts 19:6. Everts' conclusion is thus compelling: "There is really little question that in Acts 2:4 'to speak in other tongues' is a more responsible translation of λαλεῖν ἑτέραις γλώσσαις than 'to speak in other languages.'"[77]

2. LUKE-ACTS AND THE ROLE OF TONGUES IN THE CHURCH

The importance of retaining the verbal connections between the γλώσσαις (tongues) of Acts 2:4, Acts 10:46, and Acts 19:6 should not be missed. This becomes apparent when we examine Luke's understanding of the role of tongues in the life of the church.

2.1 Tongues as a Type of Prophecy

A close reading of Luke's narrative reveals that he views speaking in tongues as a special type of prophetic speech. Speaking in tongues is associated with prophecy in each of the

---

77   Ibid.

three passages that describe this phenomenon in Acts. In Acts 2:17–18 (cf. Acts 2:4), speaking in tongues is specifically described as a fulfillment of Joel's prophecy that in the last days all of God's people will prophesy. The

A close reading of Luke's narrative reveals that he views speaking in tongues as a special type of prophetic speech.

strange sounds of the disciples' tongues-speech, Peter declares, are in fact not the ramblings of drunkards; rather, they represent prophetic utterances issued by God's end-time messengers (Acts 2:13, 15–17). In Acts 19:6 the connection between prophecy and speaking in tongues is again explicitly stated. When Paul laid hands on the Ephesian disciples, the Holy Spirit "came on them, and they spoke in tongues and prophesied."

Finally, the association is made again in Acts 10:42–48. In the midst of Peter's sermon to Cornelius and his household, the Holy Spirit "came on all those who heard the message" (Acts 10:44). Peter's colleagues "were astonished that the gift of the Holy Spirit had been poured out even on the Gentiles, for they heard them speaking in tongues and praising God" (Acts 10:45–46). It is instructive to note that the Holy Spirit interrupts Peter just as he has declared, "He [Jesus] commanded us to preach to the people and to testify that he is the one whom God appointed as judge of the living and the dead. *All the prophets testify about him* that everyone who believes in him receives forgiveness of sins through his name" (Acts 10:42–43, emphasis added). In view of Luke's emphasis on prophetic inspiration throughout his two-volume work and, more specifically, his description of speaking in tongues as prophetic speech in Acts 2:17–18, it can hardly be coincidental that the Holy Spirit breaks in and inspires glossolalia precisely at this point in Peter's sermon. Indeed, as the context makes clear, Peter's colleagues are astonished at what transpires because it testifies to the fact that God has accepted uncircumcised Gentiles. Again, the connection between speaking in tongues and prophecy is crucial for Luke's narrative. In Acts 2:17–18 we are informed that reception of the Spirit of prophecy (i.e., the Pentecostal gift) is the exclusive privilege of "the servants" of God and that it typically results in miraculous and audible speech.[78] Speaking in tongues is presented as one manifestation of this miraculous, Spirit-inspired speech (Acts 2:4, 17–18). So, when Cornelius and his household burst forth in tongues, this act provides demonstrative proof that they are in fact part of the end-time prophetic band of which Joel prophesied. They too are connected to the prophets who "testify" about Jesus (Acts 10:43). This astonishes Peter's colleagues, because they recognize the clear implications that flow from this dramatic event: since Cornelius and his household are prophets, they must also be "servants" of the Lord (that is, members of the people of God). How, then, can Peter and the others withhold baptism from them (Acts 10:47–48)?

The importance of this connection in the narrative is highlighted further in Acts 11:15–18. Here, as Peter recounts the events associated with the conversion of Cornelius and his household, he emphasizes that "the Holy Spirit came on them as he had come on us at the beginning" (Acts 11:15) and then declares, "God gave them the same gift as he gave us ... " (Acts 11:17). The fact that Jewish disciples at Pentecost and Gentile believers at Caesarea

---

78   Of the eight instances where Luke describes the initial reception of the Spirit by a person or group, five specifically allude to some form of inspired speech as an immediate result (Luke 1:41; 1:67; Acts 2:4; 10:46; 19:6) and one implies the occurrence of such activity (Acts 8:15, 18). In the remaining two instances, although inspired speech is absent from Luke's account (Luke 3:22; Acts 9:17), it is a prominent feature in the pericopes that follow (Luke 4:14, 18f; Acts 9:20).

all spoke in tongues is not incidental to Luke's purposes; rather, it represents a significant theme in his story of the movement of the gospel from Jews in Jerusalem to Gentiles in Rome and beyond.

2.2 Salvation History and Tongues in Luke-Acts

Some might be tempted to suggest at this point that the special role that speaking in tongues plays as a sign in Acts 2 and Acts 10 indicates that, in Luke's view, this phenomenon was limited to these historically significant events in the early days of the founding of the church. This, however, would be to misread Luke's narrative. Luke states the point with particular clarity in Acts 2:17–21:

> [v. 17] *In the last days, God says,* [Joel: "after these things"]
> I will pour out my Spirit on all people.
> Your sons and daughters will prophesy
> *Your young men will see visions,* [Joel: these lines are inverted]
> *Your old men will dream dreams.*
> [v. 18] *Even* on *my* servants, both men and women, [additions to Joel]
> I will pour out my Spirit in those days,
> *And they will prophesy.*
> [v. 19] I will show wonders in the heaven *above*
> And *signs* on the earth *below,*
> Blood and fire and billows of smoke.
> [v. 20] The sun will be turned to darkness and the moon to blood
> Before the coming of the great and glorious day of the LORD.

[v. 21] And everyone who calls on the name of the LORD
will be saved.

(Acts 2:17–21; modifications of Joel 2:28–32 italicized)

We should remember that here Luke carefully shapes this
quotation from the LXX in order to highlight important theological
themes and truths. Three modifications are particularly striking.

First, in v. 17, Luke alters the order of the two lines that refer
to young men having visions and old men dreaming dreams. In
Joel, the old men dreaming dreams comes first. But Luke reverses
the order: "Your young men will see visions, your old men will
dream dreams" (Acts 2:17). Luke gives the reference to "visions"
pride of place in order to highlight a theme that he sees as vitally
important and that recurs throughout his narrative. Although
words associated with "dreams" are rare in Luke-Acts,[79] Luke
loves to recount stories in which God directs His church through
visions.[80] The visions of Paul and Ananias (Acts 9:10–11), of
Peter and Cornelius (Acts 10:3, 17), Paul's Macedonian vision
(Acts 16:9–10), and his vision at Corinth (Acts 18:9–10) are but a
few. Luke is not fixated on visions; rather, he seeks to encourage
his readers to embrace an important truth: God delights to lead
us, His end-time prophets, in very personal and special ways,
including visions, angelic visitations, and the prompting of the

---

79   The term translated "shall dream" is a future passive of ἐνυπνιάζω. This verb occurs only
in Acts 2:17 and in Jude 8 in the entire New Testament. The noun, ἐνύπνιον ("dream"), is
found nowhere else in Acts or the rest of the New Testament.

80   The noun translated "visions" in v. 17, ὅρασις, occurs four times in the New Testament
and only here in Acts. The other three occurrences are all found in Revelation. However,
Luke uses another term, a close cousin to ὅρασις, the neuter noun, ὅραμα, often and at
decisive points in his narrative to refer to "visions." The noun ὅραμα occurs twelve times
in the New Testament and eleven of these occurrences are found in the book of Acts (Acts
7:31; 9:10, 12; 10:3, 17, 19; 11:5; 12:9; 16:9, 10; 18:9; and then also in Matt. 17:9).

Spirit, so that we might fulfill our calling to take the gospel to "the ends of the earth."

Second, Luke inserts the phrase, "And they will prophesy," into the quotation in v. 18. It is as if Luke is saying, "whatever you do, don't miss this!" In these last days the servants of God will be anointed by the Spirit to proclaim His good news and to declare His praises. They will prophesy! This is what is *now* taking place. The speaking in tongues that you hear, declares Peter, is a fulfillment of Joel's prophecy. This special form of Spirit-inspired prophetic speech serves

> God delights to lead us, His end-time prophets, in very personal and special ways, including visions, angelic visitations, and the prompting of the Spirit, so that we might fulfill our calling to take the gospel to "the ends of the earth."

as a unique sign that "the last days" have arrived (cf. Acts 2:33–36; 10:45–46). Of course, this theme of Spirit-inspired witness runs throughout the narrative of Acts.[81]

Third, as we have previously noted, with the addition of a few words in v. 19, Luke transforms Joel's text to read: "I will show wonders in the heaven *above*, and *signs* on the earth *below*." The significance of these insertions, which form a collocation of "wonders" and "signs," becomes apparent when we look at the larger context of Acts. The first verse that follows the Joel citation declares, "Jesus . . . was a man accredited by God to you by miracles, *wonders and signs*" (Acts 2:22). And throughout the book of Acts we read of the followers of Jesus

---

81   See especially Acts 4:13, 31; 5:32; 6:10; 9:31; 13:9, 52.

working "wonders and signs." In this way, Luke links the miraculous events associated with Jesus (Acts 2:22) and His disciples (e.g., Acts 2:43) together with the cosmic portents listed by Joel (see Acts 2:19b–20) as "signs and wonders" that mark the era of fulfillment, "the last days." For Luke, "these last days"—that period inaugurated with Jesus' birth and leading up to the Day of the Lord—represents an epoch marked by "signs and wonders." According to Luke, then, visions, prophecy, and miracles—all of these should characterize the life of the church in these last days. Acts 2:17–21 indicates that Luke is conscious of the significant role that these phenomena have played in the growth of the early church and that he anticipates these activities will continue to characterize the ministry of the church in these "last days."

This conclusion, of course, has a direct bearing on the question at hand, on how we should view tongues today. As a manifestation of prophecy, Luke suggests that tongues have an ongoing role to play in the life of the church. Remember, a characteristic of "the last days"—that era of fulfillment that begins with the birth of Jesus and ends with His second coming—is that all of God's people will prophesy (Acts 2:17–18). The fact that Luke recounts various instances of the fulfillment of this prophecy that feature speaking in tongues encourages the reader to understand that, like "signs and wonders" and bold, Spirit-inspired witness for Jesus, speaking in tongues will characterize the life of the church in these last days. To suggest otherwise runs counter to Luke's explicitly stated message, not to mention that of Paul (1 Cor. 14:39).

2.3 Jesus Our Model

Luke not only views speaking in tongues as a special type of prophetic speech that has an ongoing role in the life of the church, there are also indications that he sees this form of exuberant, inspired speech modeled in the life of Jesus. Apart from the general parallels between Jesus and His disciples with reference to Spirit-inspired prophetic speech (e.g., Luke 4:18–19; Acts 2:17–18), there is a more specific parallel found in Luke 10:21, a text unique to Luke: "At that time Jesus, full of joy through the Holy Spirit, said, 'I praise you, Father, LORD of heaven and earth. . . .'"

Luke provides an interesting context for this joyful outburst of thanksgiving. It occurs in response to the return of the Seventy from their mission. As we have already noted, the sending of the Seventy (Luke 10:1, 17) echoes the prophetic anointing of the seventy elders in Numbers 11.[82] Some scholars, such as Gordon Wenham, describe the prophesying narrated in Numbers 11:24–30 as an instance of "unintelligible ecstatic utterance, what the New Testament terms speaking in tongues."[83]

On the heels of this passage, Luke describes Jesus' inspired exultation. Particularly important for our discussion is the manner in which Luke introduces Jesus' words of praise: "he rejoiced in the Holy Spirit and said" (ἠγαλλιάσατο ἐν τῷ πνεύματι τῷ ἁγίῳ καὶ εἶπεν; Luke 10:21).[84] The verb, ἀγαλλιάω (rejoice),

---

82   See also Robert P. Menzies, "The Sending of the Seventy and Luke's Purpose," in *Trajectories in the Book of Acts: Essays in Honor of John Wesley Wyckoff*, eds. Paul Alexander, Jordan D. May, and Robert Reid (Eugene, OR: Wipf & Stock, 2009), 87–113.

83   Gordon Wenham, *Numbers: An Introduction and Commentary* (Downers Grove: InterVarsity Press, 1981), 109. I am indebted to my good friend, Grant Hochman, for pointing me to this reference.

84   I am following the *American Standard Version* here for the English translation.

employed here by Luke, is used frequently in the LXX. It is usually found in the Psalms and the poetic portions of the Prophets, and it denotes spiritual exultation that issues forth in praise to God for His mighty acts.[85] The subject of the verb is not simply ushered into a state of sacred rapture; he also "declares the acts of God."[86] In the New Testament the verb is used in a similar manner. The linkage between ἀγαλλιάω and the declaration of the mighty acts of God is particularly striking in Luke-Acts.[87] The verb describes the joyful praise of Mary (Luke 1:47), Jesus (Luke 10:21), and David (Acts 2:26) in response to God's salvific activity in Jesus. In Luke 1:47 and 10:21 the verb is specifically linked to the inspiration of the Holy Spirit, and in Acts 2:25–30 David is described as a prophet. This verb, then, was for Luke a particularly appropriate way of describing prophetic activity.

> **Luke presents Jesus' Spirit-inspired prophetic ministry, including His bold proclamation and exultant praise, as a model for his readers.**

The reference in Acts 2:26 is especially interesting; for here, the verb ἀγαλλιάω is associated with the word γλῶσσα (tongue). In a quotation from Psalm 16:9 (Ps. 15:9, LXX), Peter cites David as saying, "Therefore my heart is glad and my tongue rejoices (καὶ ἠγαλλιάσατο ἡ γλῶσσά μου). . . ." This association of ἀγαλλιάω with γλῶσσα should not surprise us, for five of the eight references to γλῶσσα in Luke-Acts describe experiences of

---

85   R. Bultmann, "ἀγαλλιάομαι," *Theological Dictionary of the New Testament,* eds. Gerhard Freidrich and Gerhard Kittel (Grand Rapids: Eerdmans, 1980), vol. 1, 19; W. G. Morrice, *Joy in the New Testament* (Exeter: Paternoster Press, 1984), 20.

86   R. Bultmann, "ἀγαλλιάομαι," 20.

87   The linkage is made explicit in three out of four occurrences of the verb (Luke 1:47; 10:21; Acts 2:26). The only exception is Acts 16:34.

spiritual exultation that result in praise.[88] All of this indicates that, for Luke, ἀγαλλιάω and γλῶσσα, when associated with the inspiration of the Holy Spirit, are terms that describe special instances of prophetic inspiration, instances in which a person or group experiences spiritual exultation and, as a result, bursts forth in praise.

We conclude that Luke 10:21 describes Jesus' prayer of thanksgiving in terms reminiscent of speaking in tongues: inspired by the Spirit, Jesus bursts forth in exuberant and joyful praise. Although it is not clear that Luke's readers would have understood this outburst of inspired praise to include unintelligible utterances (i.e., glossolalia), the account does describe a relatively similar experience of spiritual rapture that produces joyful praise. What is abundantly clear is that Luke presents Jesus' Spirit-inspired prophetic ministry, including His bold proclamation and exultant praise, as a model for his readers,[89] living as they do, in these "last days."

We may summarize our argument to this point as follows:

1. Glossolalia was well known and widely practiced in the early church. Luke's references to speaking in tongues (λαλέω γλώσσαις) in Acts 10:46, 19:6, and quite possibly (but less certainly) 2:4, designate unintelligible utterances inspired by the Spirit rather than the speaking of human languages previously not learned. However we interpret this latter text (Acts 2:4), the importance of the verbal

---

88 These five include: Luke 1:64; Acts 2:4, 26; 10:46; 19:6. The other three references to γλῶσσα are found in Luke 16:24 and Acts 2:3, 11.

89 Luke's emphasis on prayer, and particularly the prayers and prayer-life of Jesus, is widely recognized by contemporary scholars. Luke also associates prayer with the Holy Spirit in a unique way (e.g., Luke 3:21–22; 11:13; Acts 4:31).

connections between the λαλέω γλώσσαις (to speak in tongues) of Acts 2:4, Acts 10:46, and Acts 19:6 should not be missed.

2. Luke's narrative reveals that he views speaking in tongues as a special type of prophetic speech. Speaking in tongues is associated with prophecy in each of the three passages that describe this phenomenon in Acts (Acts 2:4; 10:46; 19:6).

3. As a special manifestation of prophecy, Luke indicates that glossolalia has an ongoing role to play in the life of the church. This is evident from Luke's modification of Joel's prophecy in Acts 2:17–21. Here, we see that tongues serve as a sign of the arrival of the last days (Acts 2:17–21) and also of Jesus' resurrection and Lordship (Acts 2:33–36). Tongues, it should be noted, continue to serve as a demonstrable sign of reception of the prophetic gift throughout Luke's narrative (Acts 10:44–48; 19:6–7). This text (Acts 2:17–21), particularly as it is seen in the larger context of Luke-Acts, also establishes that, in Luke's perspective, speaking in tongues will continue to characterize the life of the church in these last days (that is, until Jesus returns).

4. Luke presents Jesus' experience of the Spirit and His life of prayer as important models for his readers. Luke 10:21, which describes Jesus in language reminiscent of speaking in tongues, bursting forth with Spirit-inspired, exuberant and joyful praise, is no exception.

All of this adds up to quite a resume for tongues in Luke-Acts. However, an important question still remains unanswered: Does Luke envision every believer actively engaging in glossolalia? Put another way, according to Luke, is speaking in tongues available to all? In my previous writings, I suggested that Luke does not consciously address this question. I went on to argue, however, that Paul does; and that he does so in the affirmative.[90] Nevertheless, I now believe that my judgment concerning Luke was a bit hasty. There are several texts in Luke's gospel, all unique to Luke or uniquely shaped by him, that reveal a clear intent to encourage his readers to pray for prophetic anointings, experiences that will inevitably produce bold witness and joyful praise. Luke's narrative calls for his readers to recognize that these pneumatic anointings, these experiences of spiritual rapture that issue forth in praise, are indeed available to every disciple of Jesus and that they will routinely take the form of glossolalia. To these key texts we now turn.

3. LUKE'S CHALLENGE FOR THE INDIVIDUAL BELIEVER

3.1 Luke 19:39–40

The first text we shall consider is Luke's account of Jesus' triumphal entry into Jerusalem (Luke 19:28–44), a story found in various forms in all four gospels. It is widely recognized that Luke closely follows Mark's account (Mark 11:1–10), but with one significant exception. The words of Luke 19:39–40 are unique to Luke's Gospel:

---

90   See Menzies and. Menzies, *Spirit and Power*, 121–144.

> Some of the Pharisees in the crowd said to Jesus, "Teacher, rebuke your disciples!"
> "I tell you," he replied, "if they keep quiet, the stones will cry out." (Luke 19:39–40).

At first glance the inclusion of this material in this story may not appear striking. However, when viewed in the light of Luke's emphasis on Spirit-inspired praise and witness throughout Luke-Acts, it takes on special meaning. Luke's narrative is filled with the praises of God's people, all of whom declare the mighty deeds of God. The chorus of praise begins in the infancy narratives with Elizabeth's Blessing (Luke 1:42–45), Mary's Magnificat (Luke 1:46–55), Zechariah's Song (Luke 1:67–79), and Simeon's Prophecy (Luke 2:29–32). Angels join in as well (Luke 2:13–14). The sound of Spirit-inspired praise continues with Jesus' joyful outburst (Luke 10:21–24). The angelic praise of Luke 2:13–14 is then echoed by the crowd of disciples as they welcome Jesus as He enters into Jerusalem (Luke 19:37–38). Of course in Luke 19:39–40, Luke uniquely highlights the significance of this praise. The chorus is again picked up on the day of Pentecost with the dramatic declaration of God's mighty deeds by those who have been filled with the Holy Spirit (Acts 2:1–13). It continues throughout Luke's narrative in the form of bold, Spirit-inspired witness to Jesus.[91] Irruptions of prophecy and praise are again associated with the Spirit and glossolalia in Acts 10:46 and Acts 19:6.

> **Luke's narrative is filled with the praises of God's people, all of whom declare the mighty deeds of God.**

---

91   See, for example, Acts 4:13, 31; 5:32; 6:10; 9:31; 13:9, 52.

These texts, collectively, constitute a motif that is clearly close to Luke's heart. In these last days, Luke declares, the Spirit will inspire His end-time prophets to declare God's mighty deeds, chief of which is the resurrection of Jesus. Indeed, if the disciples remain silent, "the stones will cry out!" The message to Luke's church, a church facing opposition and persecution,[92] could hardly be missed. Praise and bold witness go hand in hand, they are both the necessary and inevitable consequence of being filled with the Holy Spirit.

3.2 Luke 10:1–16

Let us now return to another text unique to Luke's Gospel, Luke's account of the Sending of the Seventy (Luke 10:1–16). While all three synoptic gospels record Jesus' words of instruction to the Twelve as He sends them out on their mission, only Luke records a second, larger sending of disciples (Luke 10:1–16). In Luke 10:1 we read, "After this the LORD appointed seventy–two [some mss. read, 'seventy'] others and sent them two by two ahead of him to every town and place where he was about to go." We have already noted that this number has symbolic significance. Jesus' selection of the Twelve was certainly not a coincidence. He did not choose twelve disciples simply because there were twelve men particularly suited for the task. The number twelve was full of symbolic meaning. It evoked the twelve sons of Jacob and thus symbolized the twelve tribes of Israel (Gen. 35:23–26).

---

92   On Luke's church as a community facing persecution, see my essay in Max Turner's *Festschrift:* Robert Menzies, "The Persecuted Prophets: A Mirror-Image of Luke's Spirit-Inspired Church," in *The Spirit and Christ in the New Testament and Christian Theology,* eds. I. Howard Marshall, Volker Rabens, and Cornelis Bennema (Grand Rapids: Wm. B. Eerdmans Publishing, 2012), 52–70.

So, Jesus' selection of the Twelve was a declaration that He was reconstituting Israel, the people of God.

We have noted that the number seventy is also rooted in the Old Testament narrative and has symbolic meaning. The background for the reference to the "seventy" is to be found in Numbers 11:24–30.[93] This passage describes how the Lord "took of the Spirit that was on [Moses] and put the Spirit on the seventy elders" (Num. 11:25). This resulted in the seventy elders, who had gathered around the Tent, prophesying for a short duration. Two other elders, Eldad and Medad, did not go to the Tent; rather, they remained in the camp and they continued to prophesy. When Joshua heard of this, he rushed to Moses and urged him to stop them. But Moses replied, "Are you jealous for my sake? I wish that all the LORD's people were prophets and that the LORD would put his Spirit on them!" (Num. 11:29).

The reference to the Seventy, then, evokes memories of Moses' wish that "all the LORD's people were prophets," and, in this way, points ahead to Pentecost (Acts 2), where this wish is initially fulfilled. Of course this wish continues to be fulfilled throughout the narrative of Acts. This reference to the Seventy, then, foreshadows the outpouring of the Spirit on all the servants of the Lord and their universal participation in the mission of God (Acts 2:17–18; cf. 4:31).[94] According to Luke, every follower of Jesus is called and promised the requisite power to be a prophet.

It is important to note that the ecstatic speech of the elders in Numbers 11 constitutes the backdrop against which Luke interprets the Pentecostal and subsequent outpourings of the

---

93   See Chapter 1 for arguments that support this conclusion.

94   Keith F. Nickle, *Preaching the Gospel of Luke: Proclaiming God's Royal Rule* (Louisville: Westminster John Knox Press, 2000), 117: "The 'Seventy' is the church in its entirety, including Luke's own community, announcing the in-breaking of God's royal rule throughout the length and breadth of God's creation."

Spirit.[95] It would appear that Luke views every believer as (at least potentially) an end-time prophet, and that he anticipates that they too will issue forth in Spirit-inspired ecstatic speech.[96] This is the clear implication of his narrative, which includes repetitive fulfillments of Moses' wish that reference glossolalia.

Of the four instances in the book of Acts where Luke actually describes the initial coming of the Spirit, three explicitly cite glossolalia as the immediate result (Acts 2:4; 10:46; 19:6) and the other one (Acts 8:14–19) strongly implies it.[97] This is the case even though Luke could have easily used other language, particularly in Acts 2, to describe what had transpired. The Acts 8 passage has various purposes. However, when it is viewed in the context of Luke's larger narrative, there can be little doubt in the reader's mind concerning the cause of Simon's ill-fated attempt to purchase the ability to dispense the Spirit. The motif is transparent; Luke's point is made: the Pentecostal gift, as

According to Luke, every follower of Jesus is called and promised the requisite power to be a prophet.

a fulfillment of Moses' wish (Num. 11:29) and Joel's prophecy (Joel 2:28–32), is a prophetic anointing that enables its recipient to bear bold witness for Jesus *and, this being the case, it is marked by the ecstatic speech characteristic of prophets* (i.e., glossolalia).

---

95 As we have noted, Gordon Wenham describes the prophesying narrated in Numbers 11:24–30 as an instance of "unintelligible ecstatic utterance, what the New Testament terms speaking in tongues" (Wenham, *Numbers*, 109).

96 With the term, *ecstatic*, I mean "pertaining to or flowing from an experience of intense joy." I do not wish to imply a loss of control with this term. While glossolalia transcends our reasoning faculties, the experience does not render them useless (cf. 1 Cor. 14:28, 32–33).

97 Paul's experience of the Spirit is not actually described (Acts 9:17–19); rather, it is implied.

This explains why Luke considered tongues to be a sign of the reception of the Pentecostal gift. Certainly Luke does present tongues as evidence of the Spirit's coming. On the day of Pentecost, Peter declares that the tongues of the disciples served as a sign. Their tongues not only established the fact that they, the disciples of Jesus, were the end-time prophets of whom Joel prophesied; their tongues also marked the arrival of the last days (Acts 2:17–21) and served to establish the fact that Jesus had risen from the dead and is Lord (Acts 2:33–36). In Acts 10:44–48, "speaking in tongues" is again "depicted as proof positive and sufficient to convince Peter's companions" that the Spirit had been poured out on the Gentiles.[98] In Acts 19:6, tongues and prophecy are cited as the immediate results of the coming of the Spirit, the incontrovertible evidence of an affirmative answer to Paul's question posed earlier in the narrative: "Did you receive the Holy Spirit when you believed?"

It is interesting to note that Luke does not share the angst of many modern Christians concerning the possibility of false tongues. Luke does not offer guidelines for discerning whether tongues are genuine or fake, from God or from some other source.[99] Rather, Luke assumes that the Christian community will know and experience that which is needed and good. This observation leads us to our next text.

---

98   James D. G. Dunn, *Jesus and the Spirit: A Study of the Religious and Charismatic Experience of Jesus and the First Christians as Reflected in the New Testament* (Philadelphia: Westminster Press, 1975), 189.

99   This sort of lacuna led James Dunn, over thirty years ago, to describe Luke's perspective as "lop-sided" (Dunn, *Jesus and the Spirit,* 191, 195). Given the dramatic rise of the Pentecostal movement and the sad state of many traditional churches, one wonders if Professor Dunn might now be more sympathetic to Luke's enthusiastic approach. Perhaps by listening more carefully to Luke the church can regain its balance.

3.3 Luke 11:9–13

Another text that reflects Luke's desire to encourage his church to experience the prophetic inspiration of the Spirit and all that it entails (i.e., joyful praise, glossolalia, and bold witness) is found in Luke 11:13. This verse, which forms the climax to Jesus' teaching on prayer, again testifies to the fact that Luke views the work of the Holy Spirit described in Acts as relevant for the life of his church. Luke is not writing wistfully about an era of charismatic activity in the distant past.[100] Luke 11:13 reads, "If you then, though you are evil, know how to give good gifts to your children, how much more will your Father in heaven give the Holy Spirit to those who ask Him!" It is instructive to note that the parallel passage in Matthew's gospel contains slightly different phrasing: "how much more will your Father in heaven give *good gifts* to those who ask Him!" (Matt. 7:11 emphasis added). It is virtually certain that Luke has interpreted the "good gifts" in his source material with a reference to the "Holy Spirit."[101] Luke, then, provides us with a Spirit-inspired, authoritative commentary on this saying of Jesus. Three important implications follow.

First, Luke's alteration of the Matthean (or Q) form of the saying anticipates the post-resurrection experience of the church.[102] This is evident from the fact that the promise that the Father will give the Holy Spirit to those who ask begins to be

---

100   Contra the judgment of Hans Conzelmann, *Acts of the Apostles* (Philadelphia: Fortress Press, 1987 [German original, 1963]), 15, 159–60.

101   Reasons for this conclusion include: (1) the fact that the reference to the Holy Spirit breaks the parallelism of the "good gifts" given by earthly fathers and "the good gifts" given by our heavenly Father; (2) Luke often inserts references to the Holy Spirit into his source material; (3) Matthew never omits or adds references to the Holy Spirit in his sources.

102   J. Fitzmyer, *The Gospel According to Luke, Vol. 2* (AB 28; New York: Doubleday, 1985), 916; E. E. Ellis, *The Gospel of Luke* (NCB; London: Oliphants, Marshall, Morgan, & Scott, 1974), 164; R. Stronstad, *The Charismatic Theology of St. Luke* (Peabody, Mass: Hendrickson, 1984), 46.

realized only at Pentecost. By contemporizing the text in this way, Luke stresses the relevance of the saying for the post-Pentecostal community to which he writes. It would seem that for Luke there is no neat line of separation dividing the apostolic church from his church or ours. Quite the contrary, Luke calls his readers to follow in their footsteps.

Second, the context indicates that the promise is made to disciples (Luke 11:1). Thus, Luke's contemporized version of the saying is clearly directed to the members of the Christian community.[103] Since it is addressed to Christians, the promise cannot refer to an initiatory or soteriological gift.[104] This judgment finds confirmation in the repetitive character of the exhortations to pray in Luke 11:9:[105] prayer for the Spirit (and, in light of the promise, we may presume this includes the reception of the Spirit) is to be an ongoing practice. The gift of the Holy Spirit to which Luke refers neither initiates one into the new age, nor is it to be received only once;[106] rather, this pneumatic gift is given to disciples and it is to be experienced on an ongoing basis (cf. Acts 2:4; 4:8, 31; 9:17; 13:9).

> **For Luke there is no neat line of separation dividing the apostolic church from his church or ours.**

---

103   The scholarly consensus affirms that Luke-Acts was addressed primarily to Christians.

104   G. T. Montague, *The Holy Spirit: Growth of a Biblical Tradition* (New York: Paulist, 1976), 259–60.

105   Note the repetitive or continuous action implicit in the verbs in 11:9: αἰτεῖτε (ask), ζητεῖτε (seek), κρούετε (knock).

106   F. Büchsel notes the repetitive character of the exhortation (*Der Geist Gottes im Neuen Testament* [Gütersloh: C. Bertlesmann, 1926], 189–90). So also Montague, *Spirit*, 259–260.

Third, Luke's usage elsewhere indicates that he viewed the gift of the Holy Spirit in 11:13 as a prophetic enabling. On two occasions in Luke-Acts the Spirit is given to those praying;[107] in both the Spirit is portrayed as the source of prophetic activity. Luke's account of Jesus' baptism indicates that Jesus received the Spirit after His baptism while praying (Luke 3:21). This gift of the Spirit, portrayed principally as the source of prophetic power (Luke 4:18–19), equipped Jesus for His messianic task. Later, in Acts 4:31, the disciples, after having prayed, "were all filled with the Holy Spirit and spoke the word of God boldly." Again the Spirit given in response to prayer is the impetus for prophetic activity.

What sort of prophetic activity did Luke anticipate would accompany this bestowal of the Spirit? Certainly a reading of Luke's narrative would suggest a wide range of possibilities: joyful praise, glossolalia, visions, and bold witness in the face of persecution, to name a few. However, several aspects of Luke's narrative suggest that glossolalia was one of the expected outcomes in Luke's mind and in the minds of his readers.

First, as we noted, Luke's narrative suggests that glossolalia typically accompanies the initial reception of the Spirit. Furthermore, Luke highlights the fact that glossolalia serves as an external sign of the prophetic gift. These elements of Luke's account would undoubtedly encourage readers in Luke's church, like they have with contemporary readers, to seek the prophetic gift, *complete with its accompanying external sign.* In short, in

---

107   Acts 8:15, 17 represents the only instance in Luke-Acts, apart from the two texts discussed above, where reception of the Spirit is explicitly associated with prayer. However, here the Spirit is bestowed on the Samaritans in response to the prayer of Peter and John. While the situation in Acts 8:15, 17 is not a true parallel to Luke 11:13, in Acts 8:15, 17 the Spirit is also portrayed in prophetic terms. Prayer is implicitly associated with the reception of the Spirit at Pentecost (Acts 1:14; 2:4). Here also the gift of the Spirit is presented as a prophetic endowment. So also Acts 9:17, though here the actual reception of the Spirit is not described.

Luke 11:13 Luke encourages his church to pray for an experience of spiritual rapture that will produce power and praise in their lives, an experience similar to those modeled by Jesus (Luke 3:21–22; 10:21) and the early church (Acts 2:4; 10:46; 19:6). The reader would naturally assume glossolalia to be a normal, frequent, and expected part of this experience.

Secondly, in view of the emphasis in this passage on asking (v. 9) and the Father's willingness to respond (v. 13), it would seem natural for Luke's readers to ask a question that again is often asked by contemporary Christians: how will we know when we have received this gift? Here we hear echoes of Paul's question in Acts 19:2. Of course, Luke has provided a clear answer. The arrival of prophetic power has a visible, external sign: glossolalia. This is not to say that there are no other ways in which the Spirit's power and presence are made known to us. This is simply to affirm that Luke's narrative indicates that a visible, external sign does exist and that he and his readers would naturally expect to manifest this sign.

I would add that this sign must have been tremendously encouraging for Luke's church, as it is for countless contemporary Christians. It signified their connection with the apostolic church and confirmed their identity as end-time prophets. I find it interesting that so many believers from traditional churches today react negatively to the notion of glossolalia as a visible sign. They often ask, should we really emphasize a visible sign like tongues? Yet these same Christians participate in a liturgical form of worship that is filled with sacraments and imagery; a form of worship that emphasizes visible signs. Signs are valuable when

The Father gives good gifts. We need not fret or fear.

they point to something significant. Luke and his church clearly understood this.

Finally, the question should be asked, why would Luke need to encourage his readers not to be afraid of receiving a bad or harmful gift (note the snake and scorpion of v. 11–12)?[108] Why would he need to encourage his church to pursue this gift of the Spirit? If the gift is quiet, internal, and ethereal, why would there be any concern? However, if the gift includes glossolalia, which is noisy, unintelligible, and has many pagan counterparts,[109] then the concern makes sense.[110] Luke's response is designed to quell any fears. The Father gives good gifts. We need not fret or fear.

In short, through his skillful editing of this saying of Jesus (Luke 11:13), Luke encourages post-Pentecostal disciples to pray for a prophetic anointing, an experience of spiritual rapture that will produce power and praise in their lives, an experience similar to those experiences modeled by Jesus (Luke 3:21–22; 10:21) and the early church (Acts 2:4; 10:46; 19:6). The reader would naturally expect glossolalia to be a normal, frequent, and expected part of this experience. The fact that Luke viewed glossolalia as a significant component of this bestowal of the Spirit is suggested by the larger context of Luke-Acts, which portrays tongues as an external sign of the Spirit's coming, and also by the

---

108   It is perhaps significant that Luke's comparisons feature dangerous objects ("snake" and "scorpion," Luke 11:11–12), whereas Matthew's comparisons include one that is simply useless ("stone" and "snake," Matt. 7:9–10). This might suggest that Luke was consciously seeking to help his readers overcome their fear.

109   For Jewish and pagan examples of ecstasy and inspired utterances see Dunn, *Jesus and the Spirit*, 304–5.

110   Note that the Beelzebub controversy immediately follows (Luke 11:14–28). Some accused Jesus of being demon-possessed (Luke 11:15). The early Christians were undoubtedly confronted with similar charges. It is thus not surprising that Luke "takes pains to show [that] Christianity [is] both different from and superior to magic" (Richard Vinson, *Luke* [Macon, GA: Smyth & Helwys Publishing, 2008], 380; cf. Acts 8:9–24; 16:16–18; 19:11–20).

more immediate context, which indicates Luke's encouragement to pray for the Holy Spirit is a response to the fears of some within his community. This text, then, indicates that Luke viewed tongues as positive and available to every disciple of Jesus.

4. CONCLUSION

I have argued that, according to Luke, tongues played a significant role in the life of the apostolic church. Furthermore, Luke expected that tongues would continue to play a positive role in his church and ours, both of which are located in "these last days." In Luke's view, every believer can manifest this spiritual gift. So, Luke encourages every believer to pray for prophetic anointings (Luke 11:13), experiences of Spirit-inspired exultation from which power and praise flow; experiences similar to those modeled by Jesus (Luke 3:21–22; 10:21) and the early church (Acts 2:4; 10:46; 19:6). Luke believed that these experiences would typically include glossolalia, which he considered a special form of prophetic speech and a sign that the Pentecostal gift had been received.

These conclusions are based on a number of interrelated arguments that might be summarized as follows:

1. Glossolalia was well known and widely practiced in the early church.
2. Luke's narrative reveals that he views speaking in tongues as a special type of prophetic speech.
3. Luke indicates that glossolalia, as a special type of prophetic speech, has an ongoing role to play in the life of the church.

4. Luke presents Jesus' experience of the Spirit and His life of prayer, including a significant moment of spiritual rapture in which He bursts forth with joyful praise (Luke 10:21), as important models for his readers.

5. Luke highlights in a unique way the importance and necessity of Spirit-inspired praise: praise and bold witness go hand in hand, as they are both the necessary and inevitable consequence of being filled with the Holy Spirit.

6. Luke views the Pentecostal outpouring of the Spirit as a fulfillment of Moses' wish (Num. 11:29) and Joel's prophecy (Joel 2:28–32). Thus, it is a prophetic anointing that is marked by the ecstatic speech characteristic of prophets (i.e. glossolalia).

7. According to Luke, the gift of tongues is available to every disciple of Jesus; thus, Luke encourages believers to pray for a prophetic anointing, which he envisions will include glossolalia.

These conclusions suggest that Luke presents a challenge to the contemporary church—a church that has all too often lost sight of its apostolic calling and charismatic roots. Glossolalia, in a unique way, symbolizes this challenge. It reminds us of our calling and our need of divine enabling. This was true of Luke's church, and it is equally true of ours. Put another way, tongues remind us of our true identity: we are to be a community of prophets, called and empowered to bear bold witness for Jesus and to declare His mighty deeds.

It should not surprise us, then, that the gift of tongues serves as an important symbol for modern Pentecostals. Just as this experience connected Luke's church with its apostolic roots, so also tongues serve a similar purpose for Pentecostals today. It symbolizes and validates our approach to the book of Acts: its stories become "our" stories. This in turn encourages us to reconsider our apostolic calling and our charismatic heritage. In short, for Pentecostals tongues serve as a sign that the calling and power of the apostolic church are valid for believers today.

EXCURSUS: CAN THOSE WHO HAVE NOT YET SPOKEN IN TONGUES EXPERIENCE PENTECOSTAL POWER?

This is a question that many of my non-Pentecostal Evangelical friends pose. They feel that Pentecostals view them as "second class" Christians. Furthermore, they insist that, by definition, any theology that speaks of a baptism in the Spirit that is distinct from conversion must ultimately lead to elitism within the church. I believe that the charge of elitism is only accurate when Pentecostals draw a necessary connection between baptism in the Spirit and Christian maturity or fruit of the Spirit, which they generally do not.[111] As we have noted, Pentecostals normally describe baptism in the Spirit as an empowering for mission. Ideally, Christian maturity and missiological power go hand in hand, but in practice we see that this is not always the case. The church at Corinth was gifted—we might say that they had charismatic power—but they were far from mature.[112] "As we walk forward in the ways of the Spirit, we will likely encounter

---

111   For more on this topic see Chapter 15, "The Baptism in the Spirit and the Fruit of the Spirit," in Menzies and Menzies, *Spirit and Power,* 201–208.

112   Compare 1 Cor. 1:5–7 with 1 Cor. 3:1–4.

moments of refreshment that are ethically transforming and missiologically inspiring. But one dimension may develop without the other."[113] Thus, Pentecostals should be quick to acknowledge that speaking in tongues is not a sign of Christian maturity. Baptism in the Spirit (in the Lukan sense) and speaking in tongues are no guarantee of a life dramatically marked by the fruit of the Spirit.

Yet, we still must address our central question: What about missiological power? Can those who have not yet spoken in tongues experience Pentecostal power? We must be very careful here not to limit God. Since we are describing experiential realities, and God delights to empower His people, it would not be wise to offer a legalistic response. In short, I do believe that many Christians who would not consider themselves to be Pentecostal and who have not spoken in tongues do experience, in varying degrees, Pentecostal power. We might call them "anonymous Pentecostals." Who can fathom the depths of the human psyche or the mind of God? Who can explain why some find it difficult to burst forth in tongues and others do not? For whatever reason, whether due to long-standing theological prejudices or one's psychological makeup, some earnest Christians find it difficult to experience this gift. I am convinced that many of these Christians

> While it may be possible to experience Pentecostal power in varying degrees without speaking in tongues, it should be noted that this is not the full biblical experience.

---

113   Menzies and Menzies, *Spirit and Power,* 207.

do experience Pentecostal power, even though they might not recognize it as such.

Here, however, I believe that it is important to qualify our response in two important ways. First, while it may be possible to experience Pentecostal power in varying degrees without speaking in tongues, it should be noted that this is not the full biblical experience. This is not Luke's Spirit-inspired intention for us. The full apostolic experience as described in Acts includes the experience of tongues. Additionally, although "anonymous Pentecostals" may experience Pentecostal power, I am also convinced that they would experience this power more frequently and to a greater extent if they consciously embraced the Pentecostal perspective. You see, Pentecostal experience is encouraged and directed by the biblical models in Acts and it is reinforced by the symbolic message of tongues. In short, there is power in the narrative and in this expressive gift (i.e., tongues). Together, they facilitate and guide our appropriation of Pentecostal power.

Let's pose the question another way: Can you be baptized in the Spirit without speaking in tongues? Perhaps. But why would we want to settle for anything less than the full apostolic experience?

Of course the pastoral issues here are real and must be addressed. What do we say to earnest Christians who have sought the Pentecostal baptism for an extended period of time (perhaps years) and still have not spoken in tongues? I would say the following: Don't allow your inability to speak in tongues to discourage you in your pursuit of God or His mission. Your lack of tongues is not a sign of immaturity or of God's displeasure. I don't know why you find it difficult to experience this gift. But I do know that speaking in tongues is only one way among many that

God encourages and edifies His children. Keep moving forward in your walk with Jesus. Stay hungry for His presence and allow Him to lead you. Follow the models in Acts. Remain open and you may yet find that He surprises you. Be encouraged by the gifts expressed within the community of faith. Rejoice with others when they speak in tongues and allow their utterances to serve as reminders of our common bond with the apostolic church. Remember that speaking in tongues is not a sign of Christian maturity nor is a lack of tongues a sign of immaturity. Above all, know that God delights to use you—and He will—for His glory.

CHAPTER FOUR

SIGNS AND WONDERS

I n 1970 James Dunn published his widely influential critique of Pentecostal theology, *Baptism in the Holy Spirit*.[114] More recently, one of Dunn's PhD students, Keith Hacking, has attempted to provide something similar for the theology of "signs and wonders" associated with the Third Wave movement. The term "Third Wave" refers to a movement of the Spirit that began in the 1980s, subsequent to the earlier Pentecostal and Charismatic movements. This "Third Wave" of the Spirit sparked a movement that was significantly impacted by John Wimber and that embraced many other conservative Evangelicals who formerly had been dispensationalists and cessationists. According to Hacking, Third Wavers present the practice of healing and exorcism, what John Wimber calls "doing the

---

114   James D. G. Dunn, *Baptism in the Holy Spirit: A Re-examination of the New Testament Teaching on the Gift of the Spirit in Relation to Pentecostalism Today* (London: SCM Press, 1970).

stuff," as ministries normative for the contemporary church. Central to Third Wave theology is not only the practice of Jesus Himself, but also the mentoring and commissioning He gave to His disciples. Third Wavers, like their Pentecostal brothers and sisters, emphasize that Jesus modeled and then commissioned His disciples to proclaim and demonstrate through signs and wonders the present-ness of the Kingdom of God. Hacking seeks to examine the purported biblical basis for these Third Wave (and we might add, Pentecostal) claims. He focuses particularly on the commissioning accounts and teaching on discipleship found in the synoptic gospels and Acts. Since Hacking's critique implicitly impacts Pentecostal belief and practice, I would like to offer a brief summary of his position and respond to it.

From the outset, Hacking's position is made clear. He chides Third Wavers for a simplistic, uncritical reading of the gospels. This "uncritical" approach is marked by two major flaws, both of which flow from the Third Wavers' relative lack of engagement with the fruit of modern biblical scholarship. First, Third Wavers tend to read the gospels as one, homogeneous whole and thus they fail to discern the distinctive theological perspective of each gospel writer. Additionally, Third Wavers fail to grasp, especially for Luke, the importance of the shift in the epochs of salvation-history, which diminishes their ability to understand the unique role of Jesus and the apostles and the miracles they wrought. In short, Hacking suggests that in the rush of their enthusiasm for things supernatural, Third Wavers have foisted their agenda upon the New Testament texts.

Hacking develops his critique by examining the commissioning accounts and teaching on discipleship found in Matthew, Mark, and then Luke-Acts. Matthew, we are told, presents Jesus as a Mosaic prophet who rightly interprets the law. Jesus passes on His "authority to teach" to the disciples and this constitutes the "heart of the Great Commission."[115] Hacking grudgingly acknowledges that the "authority" that Jesus confers on the disciples might also include authority over the demonic, but he insists that Matthew places far greater emphasis on authority to forgive sins, as well as to teach. Hacking concludes that Matthew's teaching on discipleship, which includes the important themes of suffering and persecution, the necessity of forgiveness, and the discipline of righteous living, indicates that the working of "signs and wonders" was not a particularly important dimension of Christian discipleship for Matthew. One is only left to wonder, particularly in light of Matthew's clear association of "authority" and charismatic ministry (e.g., Matt. 9:8; 10:1; 28:18), if Matthew and his community really felt that these obviously important themes and an emphasis on signs and wonders were mutually exclusive.

Mark too presents a rich picture of Christian discipleship, one that concentrates on much more than simply the ability to perform miracles. The weighty matters of discipleship are taken up by Mark in his central section. Here Mark teaches by describing the blunders of the disciples on the one hand, and the corrective teaching of Jesus on the other. Discipleship for Mark centers on "utter commitment, a servant spirit, willingness to suffer and a focus . . . on doing the will of God."[116] Additionally, Hacking suggests that the commissioning of the disciples to perform healings and exorcisms is not aimed at the entire Christian community but, rather, applies only to Christians engaged in pioneer missionary activity.

---

115   Keith J. Hacking, *Signs and Wonders, Then and Now: Miracle-working, Commissioning and Discipleship* (Nottingham: Apollos/IVP, 2006), 100.

116   Hacking, *Signs and Wonders*, 152.

This conclusion creates a tension with Hacking's earlier statement that "Discipleship for Mark has mission as its purpose."[117] This tension is not resolved but intensified when we realize that the central section of Mark's gospel includes a story about the disciples' inability to exorcise a demon (Mark 9:14–29). After an implicit rebuke ("O unbelieving generation . . . how long shall I put up with you!"), Jesus exorcises the demon and then instructs the disciples concerning how these kinds of demons are to be cast out. Elsewhere in the central section, this sort of misunderstanding and correction is cited by Hacking as Mark's method of instruction. On the basis of Hacking's earlier conclusions, one would envision that here Mark is instructing his church concerning the proper method of and approach to exorcism. Not so, declares Hacking. In an interesting bit of reverse logic, Hacking concludes that the story teaches "that the earlier spectacular successes on the part of the disciples sent out by Jesus in mission should not be regarded by Mark's readers as the everyday norm for the church."[118] This puzzling hermeneutical shift continues with Hacking's analysis of Mark 9:38–41, which describes Jesus' correction of John, who is peeved that someone apart from the Twelve was casting out demons. Jesus declares, "Do not stop him. . . . No one who does a miracle in my name can in the next moment say anything bad about me, for whoever is not against us is for us. I tell you the truth, anyone who gives you a cup of water in my name because you belong to Christ will certainly not lose his reward" (Mark 9:39–41). It would appear that this story, which has impressive parallels to Numbers 11:26–29, encourages the Twelve and, by extension, Mark's church, *not* to limit the casting out of demons to a select few. Yet Hacking gleans something rather

---

117   Ibid., 112.

118   Ibid., 130.

different from this text. According to Hacking, the story teaches that "exorcism in Jesus' name need not necessarily involve (true) discipleship and, as such, should be regarded by his readers as being of relatively minor importance."[119]

Hacking's treatment of Luke-Acts, which is especially crucial for our purposes, follows a pattern that has now become rather predictable. First, he argues that Luke does not present Jesus' reception of the Spirit as a model for later disciples. This is the case in spite of overwhelming evidence to the contrary. Hacking ignores the fact that Luke has crafted his narrative in such a way as to stress the parallels between Jesus' reception of the Spirit at the Jordan and the disciples' reception of the Spirit at Pentecost: both receptions take place at the outset of their respective ministries; both experiences are accompanied by visible manifestations; both are interpreted as a fulfillment of Old Testament prophecy in the context of a sermon that closely follows the event. Hacking's judgment at this point is impaired by his tendency to accept the notion that Luke has a rigid, fragmented view of salvation-history. Conzelmann's three-epoch view was discredited long ago, but Hacking still operates with a slightly modified version of Conzelmann's scheme. Martin Hengel gave voice to a virtual consensus in Lukan scholarship when he wrote some years ago that Conzelmann's

> **Luke has crafted his narrative in such a way as to stress the parallels between Jesus' reception of the Spirit at the Jordan and the disciples' reception of the Spirit at Pentecost.**

---

119   Ibid., 133.

view "that Luke divides history up into three periods . . . was nevertheless misleading. . . . In reality, the whole double work covers the one history of Jesus Christ, which . . . includes the interval between resurrection and parousia as the time of his proclamation in the 'last days' (Acts 2:17)."[120]

Unfortunately, this faulty presupposition also encourages Hacking to emphasize discontinuity between the charismatic ministry of Jesus and the apostles on the one hand, and ministry in Luke's church and ours on the other. Hacking frequently argues for the uniqueness of the miracles of Jesus and the apostles. He states, "signs and wonders in Acts are to be understood as being instrumental in the formation of the infant church."[121] Hacking builds on this by arguing that Luke restricts signs and wonders to a chosen few, a select group of designated individuals who are set apart and commissioned, initially by Jesus, but later by their local congregations. He concludes, "Luke associated signs and wonders only with those who had a transparently authoritative role to play in the missiological progress of the church."[122]

Yet these conclusions again run counter to the evidence from Luke-Acts. The sending of the seventy-two (Luke 10:1–16) is a case in point. Hacking argues that the instructions given to the seventy-two, which include "heal the sick" (Luke 11:9; cf. 11:17), were limited to the earthly ministry of Jesus and were "not intended by Luke to provide an ongoing contemporary paradigm."[123] However, as we have already noted, this text has important parallels to Numbers 11:24–29 and should be read

---

120   Martin Hengel, *Acts and the History of Earliest Christianity,* trans. J. Bowden (London: SCM Press, 1979), 59.

121   Hacking, *Signs and Wonders,* 257.

122   Ibid.

123   Ibid., 195.

with Moses' declaration, "I wish that all the LORD's people were prophets" (Num. 11:29), in mind. The manuscript evidence, divided as it is between a sending out of seventy or seventy-two, attests to the fact that the early church understood the text in this way. The actual number of the elders who were anointed in Numbers 11 is somewhat ambiguous, depending on whether or not Eldad and Medad are included in the original seventy. This accounts for later scribal discrepancies. This passage then, which expands the group of empowered disciples beyond the Twelve and echoes Moses' wish for a prophethood of believers, finds its fulfillment in the Pentecostal outpouring of the Spirit.

Luke's concern to encourage his church to see the Pentecostal gift of the Spirit and the charismatic power that it provides as available to every believer is further emphasized in Luke 11:9–13 (par. Matt. 7:7–11), where Luke alters the Q version of the saying to read "Holy Spirit" rather than "good gifts." Luke's redacted version of this saying ("how much more will your Father in heaven give the Holy Spirit to those who ask him!") obviously anticipates the post-Easter experience of the church, since the gift of the Spirit was not bestowed until Pentecost. By contemporizing the text in this way, Luke stresses the relevance of the saying for the post-Pentecostal community to which he writes. He crafts his narrative so as to encourage his church—indeed, the *entire* church—to pray that they, too, might be empowered by the Pentecostal gift.

Finally, Luke could hardly have stated the matter more clearly than he does in Peter's sermon at Pentecost (see especially Acts 2:17–22). Peter declares to the amazed crowd that the events of Pentecost that they have just witnessed represent the fulfillment of Joel 2:28–32. The universality of the promise is highlighted in Acts 2:17–18 with the reference to "all people" and the poetic couplets that follow (sons/daughters; young men/old men; men/women). The point is unequivocal: in the last days the Lord will pour out the Spirit on *all* of God's servants.

Equally important for this discussion is Luke's alteration of Joel's text in Acts 2:19. We have already noted that with the addition of a few words, Luke transforms Joel's text to read: "I will show wonders in the heaven *above*, and *signs* on the earth *below*." The significance of these insertions, which places "wonders" together with "signs," becomes apparent when we read the first verse that follows the Joel citation, "Jesus . . . was a man accredited by God to you by miracles, *wonders and signs*" (Acts 2:22). The subsequent narrative of Acts highlights the fact that the followers of Jesus also perform "wonders and signs."

> The point is unequivocal: in the last days the Lord will pour out the Spirit on *all* of God's servants.

In this way, Luke presents the miracles associated with Jesus and His disciples as a partial fulfillment of Joel's prophecy of cosmic signs (see Acts 2:19b–20). These cosmic signs distinguish the era of fulfillment, "the last days." For Luke, "these last days"—that period inaugurated with Jesus' birth and consummated with His second coming—represents an era marked by "signs and wonders." Luke, then, not only highlights the significant role that miracles had played in the past; he also declares that "signs and wonders" will characterize the ministry of the church in the future. Indeed, according to Luke, we should expect "signs and wonders" to mark the life of the church until the consummation of God's great plan of salvation.

Nevertheless, in spite of all of this, Hacking seeks to argue that Luke restricts the working of miracles to the apostles and a few heroes of the Spirit who received special commissions. Yet the very fact that Hacking has to expand the "limited" group beyond the apostles to other heroes of the Spirit should give the reader pause. Other questions emerge as well: Are we really to understand the prayer of Acts 4:29–30 ("Enable your servants to speak your word with great boldness. Stretch out your hand to heal and perform miraculous signs and wonders. . . .") as limited to a select few? Philip was commissioned to help with the distribution of food, not pioneer churches, and yet miraculous signs accompany his proclamation in Samaria (Acts 8:6). How does this fit with Hacking's thesis? And, apart from the apostles and other heroes of the Spirit, what other characters could Luke use to make his point?

In short, Hacking raises interesting and important questions concerning the theology of "signs and wonders." His discussion of discipleship material in the synoptic Gospels and Acts is often insightful and inspiring. Furthermore, he demonstrates that the gospel writers were not fixated on charismatic power, nor were they uncritical in their approach to the miraculous. But key aspects of his thesis—that the gospel writers were largely uninterested in "signs and wonders" as a significant component of Christian discipleship, that the miracles of Jesus and the apostles were not intended to serve as models for the post-apostolic church, and that the commissioning accounts are relevant to only a select few who are specifically commissioned to engage in pioneer work—appear to be built on a selective reading of the text and faulty presuppositions.

Yet Hacking's question cannot be ignored: Should every believer expect to see "signs and wonders" as a part of his or her Christian life and witness? I have no doubt how the vast majority of my Christian friends in China would answer this question.

And a recent survey of Pentecostals from ten different nations concludes that an extremely high percentage claim to have personally witnessed or experienced instances of divine healing (87 percent in Kenya, 79 percent in Nigeria, 77 percent in Brazil, 74 percent in India, 72 percent in the Philippines, 62 percent in the US).[124] Perhaps it is time for those of us from increasingly secular countries to learn from our brothers and sisters in the Two-thirds World. After all, aren't their cultures often closer to that of the biblical authors than our own?

> **Pentecostals proclaim a God who is near, a God whose power can and should be experienced here and now.**

It seems to me that their experiences and perspectives point to significant weaknesses in the presuppositions that often guide the interpretative paradigms of scholars in Europe and North America.

I am thankful that Pentecostals the world over celebrate the present-ness of the Kingdom of God. God's awesome presence in our midst, His gracious willingness to bestow spiritual gifts, His desire to heal, liberate, and transform lives—all of these themes, so central to Pentecostal piety, highlight the fact that God's reign is now present. Pentecostals proclaim a God who is near, a God whose power can and should be experienced here and now. This element of Pentecostal praxis has, for the most part, served as a much-needed corrective to traditional church life, which has far too often lost sight of the manifest presence of God. Here, again, Pentecostals have a rich legacy to pass on.

---

124   See the Pew Forum Survey at http://pewforum. org/surveys/pentecostal.

CHAPTER FIVE

WHY PENTECOSTAL CHURCHES ARE GROWING

I n 2009 the University of Southern California established the Pentecostal and Charismatic Research Initiative (PCRI) with a $6.9 million grant from the John Templeton Foundation. In a news release dated February 24, 2009, PCRI spokesperson Donald Miller states, "We are interested in why Pentecostalism is growing so rapidly, what impact it is having on society, and how it is different in various cultural settings."[125] The initiative will "foster innovative social science research in Africa, Asia, Latin America and the former Soviet Union, by providing up to $3.5 million in grants."[126] While I applaud this worthy project and wish all of the researchers associated with it well, I must admit that in my less charitable moments I wonder how valuable and helpful the information gleaned from this research will be in answering the central question: Why are Pentecostal

---

125   See Miller's comments at www.usc.edu/uscnews/newsroom/news_release.php?id=558.

126   Ibid.

churches growing? My skepticism is rooted in the fact that this initiative appears to intentionally ignore or, at best, minimize the theological dimension of the Pentecostal movement and seeks to answer this important question largely in sociological terms. This sort of reductionistic approach seems destined to provide, at best, limited, and possibly even distorted, results. It is akin to studying why birds can fly, without considering their feathers.

Lest I be misunderstood, let me say that I do believe that the PCRI will provide interesting, and in many cases valuable, data. It will undoubtedly illuminate some of the cultural trends that have facilitated the rise of the Pentecostal movement around the world. However, if the central question really focuses on why Pentecostal churches are growing, then I would suggest that the PCRI should have spent a good portion of their money inquiring into the biblical ethos and theological values that shape the Pentecostal movement. Now, I am not so bold as to suggest that my own attempt to answer this question in the following pages will yield results as comprehensive and nuanced as the combined wisdom of the sociological research; however, I would note that my wisdom on this matter comes at a fraction of the cost. In fact, I do believe that I might have something unique to offer. The reason for this bold claim is simple: sociology can help us describe the "what," but it struggles to help us understand the "why." I believe this is particularly true of the rise of the modern Pentecostal movement, which points beyond human horizons to a God who delights to work in and through us.

If we are to understand why Pentecostal churches are growing, we above all will need to understand what Pentecostal Christians believe, what energizes their lives and witness, what sets them apart and makes them unique. In short, we need to understand why Pentecostals are different. It is this "why" question that inevitably takes us back to the question of belief, to the theological values of grass-roots, ordinary believers. My father was fond of highlighting the fact that theology, experience, and behavior are all interrelated. What we believe is impacted by, but also guides, our experience. Our beliefs give meaning, coherence, and direction to our experience; and in this way, impact and shape our behavior.

This recognition of the interconnectedness of our beliefs, experience, and behavior leads me to insist that Pentecostal convictions are an essential part of Pentecostal experience and praxis. We cannot speak of one as if it were totally independent of the others. For this reason, I believe that the question of why Pentecostal churches are growing is at its heart a theological question. Indeed, I am convinced that there are five theologically-oriented reasons for the unique and rapid growth of the modern Pentecostal movement. Without taking into account these core convictions, which are shared by Pentecostals around the world, one cannot provide an adequate answer to our central question. Let us examine, then, the five characteristics and related convictions that drive this influential and growing movement forward.

Our beliefs give meaning, coherence, and direction to our experience; and in this way, impact and shape our behavior.

1. MISSIONAL DNA

Pentecostal experience and praxis are shaped, in large measure, by the stories contained in the book of Acts. The central texts that Pentecostals around the world memorize and feature are

Acts 1:8, "But you will receive power when the Holy Spirit comes on you; and you will be my witnesses in Jerusalem, and in all Judea and Samaria, and to the ends of the earth," and Acts 2:4, "All of them were filled with the Holy Spirit and began to speak in other tongues as the Spirit enabled them." These texts and the related stories of bold missionary endeavor that follow in the book of Acts provide the templates for our understanding of baptism in the Spirit. They shape Pentecostal experience and give direction to our mission. Within the larger Christian family this emphasis is unique and it gives the Pentecostal movement a profoundly missional ethos. This is, in my opinion, one of the key reasons why Pentecostal churches are growing. It is certainly a central reason why scores of missionaries, most with meager financial backing, left the Azusa Street Revival and traveled to diverse points of the globe to proclaim the "apostolic" faith. I would suggest it is also why Pentecostals today constantly share their faith with others. Bold witness for Jesus is recognized as our primary calling and the central purpose of our experience of the Spirit's power. Missions is woven into the fabric of our DNA.

This perspective, this missiological emphasis gleaned from Luke-Acts, is unique to Pentecostals. While Pentecostals have featured Luke's Gospel and the book of Acts, other Protestant churches have highlighted the Pauline epistles. The great truths of the Reformation were largely gleaned from Romans and Galatians and the other writings of Paul. The terminology "justification by faith" echoes Paul. So, following the lead of Luther, Calvin, and the other reformers, the Protestant churches have largely emphasized the Pauline epistles as their core texts.

This Pauline emphasis has, to a large extent, shaped the Evangelical movement. Elsewhere I have outlined how Evangelicals, in a knee-jerk reaction to liberal scholarship that challenged the historical reliability of Luke's writings, rejected the notion that Luke was a theologian.[127] Evangelicals maintained that Luke and the other Gospel writers were *not* theologians; they were historians. In Evangelical circles any discussion of the theological purpose of Luke and his narrative was muted. The Gospels and Acts were viewed as historical records, not accounts reflecting self-conscious theological concerns. Of course this approach essentially created a canon within the cannon and, by giving Paul pride of place as the "theologian" of the New Testament, had a significant Paulinizing effect on Evangelical theology. Evangelicals are just now beginning to come to terms with the theological significance of the biblical narratives.

Pentecostals affirm that every disciple is called and empowered and every disciple is encouraged to expect that "signs and wonders" will accompany his or her witness.

Certainly Evangelicals have, in their own way, highlighted the missionary call. Generally this has come by way of the Great Commission in Matthew 28:18–20. This text has perhaps been more acceptable to Evangelicals than the commissioning material in Acts, since here Jesus is the One who has "all authority" and there is no overt commission for His disciples to work "signs and wonders." Yet, even here, tensions persist. Is this commission valid for everyone in the church? And how does Jesus' authority relate to the disciples He sends out? Here the Pentecostal reading of Acts provides clear and ready answers. On the basis of their reading of Acts, Pentecostals affirm that every disciple is called

---

127   See Menzies and Menzies, *Spirit and Power*, 37–45.

and empowered and every disciple is encouraged to expect that "signs and wonders" will accompany his or her witness. Evangelicals tend to be, at best, less clear on these matters.

More recently, Third Wave Evangelicals have highlighted the role of spiritual gifts in evangelism.[128] But, as I have pointed out elsewhere, this perspective, rooted as it is in Paul's gift language, fails to offer a solid rationale for a high sense of expectancy with respect to divine enabling.[129] When it comes to spiritual gifts, the attitude of many is quite passive. Perhaps verbal witness is not our gift. What is lacking here is a clear promise of empowering that extends to every believer. Pentecostals find this in the narrative of Acts (Acts 1:8; 2:19). Furthermore, Luke highlights more than simply "signs and wonders." His narrative is also filled with examples of bold, Spirit-inspired witness in the face of opposition and persecution (e.g., Luke 12:11–12; Acts 4:31). This staying power is an undisputable focus in Luke's narrative, and it has been central to Pentecostal missions as well. Here again we need to hear Luke's unique contribution.

I do not wish to minimize in any way the significance of the great doctrinal truths of Paul's writings. I merely point out that since Paul was, for the most part, addressing specific needs in various churches, his writings tend to feature the inner life of the Christian community. His writings, with some significant exceptions, do not focus on the mission of the church to the world. So, for example, Paul has much to say about spiritual gifts and how they should be exercised in corporate worship (1 Cor. 12–14); however, he is relatively silent when it comes to the Pentecostal outpouring of the Spirit. It is probably fair to say that

---

128   See for example John Wimber and Kevin Springer, *Power Evangelism* (San Francisco: Harper & Row, 1991).

129   Menzies and Menzies, *Spirit and Power,* 145–58.

while Paul features the "interior" work of the Spirit (e.g., the fruit of the Spirit, Gal. 5:22–23); Luke features His "expressive" work (Acts 1:8). Thus, by appropriating in a unique way the significant contributions of Luke-Acts, Pentecostals have developed a piety with a uniquely outward or missiological thrust.

This Lukan and missiological emphasis, transmitted largely through the stories in the book of Acts, also points to a significant difference that distinguishes the Pentecostal movement from the Charismatic movement. Whereas the Pentecostal movement from the beginning has been a missionary movement, the Charismatic movement has largely been a movement of spiritual renewal within existing, mainline churches. Here, the names are instructive. The term *Pentecostal* points us to Pentecost and the missionary call and power that is given to the church (Acts 1–2). The term *Charismatic*, by way of contrast, points to the spiritual gifts that serve to edify the church, particularly as it gathers together for corporate worship (1 Cor. 12–14). Both movements have blessed the wider church and brought fresh insights and much-needed spiritual energy. However, the missiological legacy of the Pentecostal movement is conspicuous. The same cannot be said for the Charismatic movement.

Their unique appropriation of Luke-Acts not only distinguishes Pentecostals from their Evangelical and Charismatic brothers and sisters, it also highlights a significant difference that separates them from the liberal wing of the Protestant church. It should be noted that many liberals, unlike their Evangelical counterparts, have given more attention to the Gospels, and particularly to Jesus, than to Paul. In fact, some liberals go so far as to claim that Paul distorted or obscured the "pure" teachings of Jesus. It would appear, at least with this emphasis on the gospel narratives, that liberals and Pentecostals might find some common ground. But here again we encounter a major difference. Whereas liberals seek to understand Jesus in the light of a critical scholarship that discounts the possibility of the miraculous, Pentecostals, without hesitation, embrace the miracle-working Jesus of the New Testament who is both fully human and fully divine. The difference is profound. One has an apostolic faith to proclaim. The other is left with little but pious platitudes. Again, it is not difficult to see why one is a missionary movement and the other is not.

2. A CLEAR MESSAGE

Pentecostals, largely because of their unwavering commitment to the Bible and particularly the book of Acts, have a clear and uncomplicated message. The message of the apostles is also their message: Jesus is Lord and Savior. The simple message that "salvation is found in no one else" (Acts 4:12), only in Jesus, shines brightly in a world full of relativism, moral chaos, and spiritual darkness. Indeed, as sociologist David Martin notes, Pentecostals are having a tremendous impact among the poor of Latin America precisely because of the clarity of their message.

> **Pentecostals are having a tremendous impact among the poor of Latin America precisely because of the clarity of their message.**

With reference to the challenges facing poor families in Brazil, which are often ravaged by the pull of "a culture of machismo, drink, sexual conquest, and carnival," he writes: "It is a contest between the home and the street, and what restores the home is the discontinuity and inner transformation offered by a demanding, disciplined faith with firm boundaries."[130]

The clarity of the Pentecostal message flows from the simple, straightforward manner in which we read the Bible. As I have noted, Pentecostals love the stories of the Bible. We identify with the stories that fill the pages of the Gospels and Acts, and the lessons gleaned from these stories are easily grasped and applied in our lives. For Pentecostals, the New Testament presents models that are to be emulated and guidelines that are to be followed.

It should be noted that our approach to doing theology is not dependent on mastering a particular set of writings, say, the works of Luther; or coming to terms with a highly complex theological system. Pentecostals also do not worry much about cultural distance or theological diversity within the canon. We do not lose sleep over how we should understand the miracle stories of the Bible or how we might resolve apparent contradictions in the Bible. Our commitment to the Bible as the Word of God enables us to face these questions with a sense of confidence. Furthermore, our experience of God's presence serves as a constant reminder that calls us back to the basic purpose of our reading in the first place: to know God and His will for our lives more clearly. Finally, our sense of connection with the apostolic church and its mission, encouraged by the similarities between our experiences and those described in the biblical text, call us to focus on the challenge before us. Though we know that Jesus is the victor, the battle still rages. We have been called to serve as Jesus' end-time prophets. So we read with purpose. Their stories are our stories.

---

130   David Martin, *Pentecostalism: The World Their Parish* (Oxford: Blackwell, 2002), 106; prior quote from 105.

In a world still populated by a huge number of illiterate or semi-literate people, the simplicity of the Pentecostal approach, rooted as it is in the biblical narrative, is often appreciated. The stories of the Bible and the stories of personal testimony often play an important role in Pentecostal worship and instruction. These stories make the communication of the message much easier, especially when cultural barriers need to be hurdled. This is particularly so when the stories connect with the felt needs of the hearers, as is generally the case with stories of spiritual deliverance, physical healing, and moral transformation. Most of the people who inhabit our world believe in God (or at least gods) and spiritual power. They simply do not know Him. They usually do, however, have a clear sense of their needs. In our world, a narrative approach that takes seriously the spiritual needs of people and the miraculous power of God is destined to win a hearing.

I would also add that, in accordance with the record of apostolic ministry contained in the book of Acts, Pentecostals have focused their attention on proclaiming the gospel and not on political or social action. This is not to say that Pentecostals have not had a significant social impact. On the contrary, Pentecostals around the world are the church of the poor and their virtues of "betterment, self-discipline, aspiration, and hard work," nurtured by the life-transforming power of the Spirit experienced in the community of believers, enable this often marginalized group to survive and prosper. As David Martin aptly notes, "Pentecostals belong to groups which liberals cast in the role of victim, and in every way they refuse to play that role."[131] Although it often goes unrecognized, Pentecostals around the

---

131   Martin, *Pentecostalism,* 10. Prior quote also from 10.

globe are having a dramatic social impact. But they are doing so precisely because they are focused on a clear biblical message of repentance, forgiveness, and transformation. This message builds worshipping communities that embody and foster virtues that build families, empower women, nurture children, and enable the poor to prosper.[132]

The people who talk the most about helping the poor are generally not the poor. They also frequently lack the spiritual resources necessary to deal with the fundamental issues that confront the poor. In the contest between the home and the street, more is needed than helpful instruction and handouts. Nothing less than the transforming power of God's presence is needed to foster the individual discipline and build the caring community required to win this battle. This is exactly what Pentecostals feature. Their approach is not the result of detailed sociological analysis or demographic studies. It does not flow from the pages of numerous case studies or the reports of well-heeled relief agencies. Rather, their approach flows from the book of Acts. By and large, Pentecostals do what Graham Twelftree suggests was the practice of the early church: they preach and demonstrate with signs and wonders the gospel to those outside the church; and they apply social justice within the church.[133]

---

132   For an objective but positive assessment, see Martin, *Pentecostalism.*

133   Graham H. Twelftree, *People of the Spirit: Exploring Luke's View of the Church* (Grand Rapids: Baker Academic, 2009), 203. Twelftree concludes, "Social action, in terms of caring for the physical needs of the outsider, plays no part in Luke's view of mission" (203). On the priority of proclamation over social action in Luke's view of mission, see also Robert Menzies, "Complete Evangelism: A Review Essay," *Journal of Pentecostal Theology* 13 (1998), 133–42. More affluent Pentecostals are beginning to engage in a variety of creative approaches that enable them to connect with non-Christians, including business enterprises and social programs. Whether they will be able to maintain their historic focus on the priority of sharing the gospel and making disciples remains to be seen. Since, from a Pentecostal perspective, the gospel is our most precious gift, I would suggest that love demands nothing less.

This approach has the advantage of featuring a message that clearly centers on the Word of God and thus serves to unite the community of faith. The farther afield the church moves into the realm of political or social action, the less it is able to speak with clarity about its suggested course of action. Should Christians support a welfare state as a compassionate choice for the poor? Or should they encourage less government intervention so that individuals and churches have more freedom and resources to minister to them? These are the kind of questions that individual Christians often consider. However, because these questions are not directly dealt with in the Scriptures, they normally generate conflicting responses. Pentecostals have, for the most part, avoided theological reflection and philosophical speculation that takes the church away from its apostolic foundations and its central truths. They show little interest in political theology or interfaith dialogue. Some may see this as a weakness, but I think history has shown that it is a great strength.

3. SIGNS AND WONDERS

Pentecostals routinely pray for the sick and take seriously the commission of Jesus to preach the good news and heal the sick. Again, the record of Acts is crucial, for the signs and wonders of the apostolic church form models for our contemporary practice. The impact of this approach is hard to miss.

One recent study of a Pentecostal group in Brazil, cited by Martin, found that almost half of the female converts and roughly a quarter of the male converts came to conversion through illness. "Pentecostals seek out those in need where they are, and the need is often signaled by illness." The study noted how the locals faced "all the maladies of poverty from worms and parasites to dehydration and undernourishment, from snakebite to ovarian cancer." In this context, prayer for healing takes on special significance. Martin eloquently describes the typical Pentecostal convert as "someone who has restored the home, holds the Bible fiercely in hand, and finds in the Holy Spirit the ecstatic lover of the soul and healer of body. For those whose words are discounted in the wider world He gives the Word as well as the tongue to express it."[134]

My own experience also confirms the important role that prayer for the sick plays in the growth of the Pentecostal church. On one occasion I attended a meeting of a house church in a large Chinese city. I traveled to the meeting with an American Christian who described himself as a "mild cessationist." We arrived at the designated apartment early and noted that a group of five or six ladies had already arrived. My friend was curious about their stories and asked me, "How did these ladies become Christians?" So I said, "Let's ask them." I proceeded to translate the ladies' responses to our question. Each one of the ladies referred to a miracle of healing, either in their own lives or in the life of a family member, as they described their journey to faith in Christ. In China this is by no means unusual, but rather, the norm.

The signs and wonders of the apostolic church form models for our contemporary practice.

The significance of this Pentecostal emphasis on prayer for the sick should not be minimized. Historically, Christianity has often expressed ambiguous and, at times, sub-biblical attitudes toward the body. The Gnostic tendency to view the body as evil

---

134   Martin, *Pentecostalism*, 106. Prior quotes from 105–6.

and a prison of the soul has too often influenced the church. The result has been an emphasis on "the saving of souls" with little concern for the body and the concrete, physical needs of people here and now. Yet Pentecostals declare a different message. While Pentecostals are careful not to downplay humanity's desperate need for forgiveness and moral transformation through the Spirit, they also boldly proclaim that Jesus is the Healer.

Pentecostals insist that divine healing is a sign of the presence of the Kingdom of God and that it should not be a rare and unusual experience limited to a select few. They call every believer to live with a sense of expectancy, recognizing that Jesus delights to bestow gifts of healing and bring physical wholeness to His people.

This holistic understanding of humanity also enables Pentecostals to relate the gospel directly to the matter of material need. For example, David Yonggi Cho declares that God is a good God and as such, He wants to bestow upon us material, as well as spiritual and physical, blessings. Cho encourages believers to "lay aside the thinking that spiritual blessings and heaven are all we need, and that material blessings are out of place for us."[135] Although some have criticized Cho for proclaiming what they believe to be an unbiblical "prosperity gospel," I believe Allan Anderson's words of warning need to be heard:

> It is important to realize that Cho did not develop his teaching on success and prosperity from the context of the affluent West and the North American "health and wealth" preachers . . . it was in the context of the slums of Seoul among people recovering from the horrors of

---

135   David Yonggi Cho, *Salvation, Health, and Prosperity: Our Threefold Blessings in Christ* (Altamonte Springs, FL: Creation House, 1987), 54–55.

the Japanese occupation and the Korean War when Cho began to preach that poverty was a curse.[136]

Additionally, it should be noted that Cho's message is solidly Christocentric, centering on Jesus and His redemptive work.[137] This focus on Jesus and living in order to glorify Him brings balance to Cho's message. "We must remember," admonishes Cho, "that whatever we do, God is measuring the work we do for Him in a qualitative, not quantitative way.... Only the work which is done by the power of the Holy Spirit can be acceptable in the Kingdom of God."[138] Indeed, for Cho, material blessing is inseparably related to mission. Cho declares, "We are in God's business. We are in business to make a profit, not in money, but in souls."[139] This outward, service-oriented focus separates Cho's discussion about prosperity from a self-centered hedonism. And, while Cho highlights God's desire to bless his people, he also speaks of the necessity of persevering through suffering and hardship: "Many people think that when you have faith, everything will flow easily, with few problems encountered. But it is important to remember that this is not so."[140] In fact, Cho sees suffering as the pathway to spiritual growth. He writes, "The deeper our faith becomes, the more we have experiences that challenge us to allow God to

---

136   Allan Anderson, "The Contextual Pentecostal Theology of David Yonggi Cho" in *David Yonggi Cho: A Close Look at His Theology and Ministry,* eds. W. Ma, W. Menzies, and H. Bae (*Asian Journal of Pentecostal Studies* 7, no. 1 [Baguio: APTS Press, 2004]), 155.

137   See Anderson, "David Yonggi Cho," 154.

138   Yonggi Cho, *The Fourth Dimension, Volume Two: More Secrets for a Successful Faith Life* (Plainfield: Bridge Publishing, 1983), 16.

139   Yonggi Cho, *Fourth Dimension, Volume Two,* 2.

140   Paul Yonggi Cho, *The Fourth Dimension: The Key to Putting Your Faith to Work for a Successful Life* (Plainfield: Logos, 1979), 140.

break us, but the more we experience brokenness, the deeper our faith becomes."[141]

The Pentecostal message, then, centers on the all-embracing salvation found in Jesus. It is designed to encourage faith and bring hope to people living in the midst of hopelessness and despair. And Pentecostals do not hesitate to relate the gospel to the whole spectrum of human need, whether it be spiritual, physical, or material. This holistic approach is a refreshing correction to traditional theologies that ignore the body and its needs. Ulrich Luz's perceptive comments concerning Paul's "theology of glory" might be aptly applied to the holistic theology of Pentecostalism as well. Luz notes that "the fear and panic at 'enthusiasm' and any *theologia gloriae* which marks out many Protestant theologians is unknown to Paul, for it is not a question of his own glory, but Christ's."[142]

4. LIMITED CHURCH STRUCTURE

Pentecostal churches tend to be congregational in polity and they do not have established or strict academic prerequisites for church leadership. This means that leaders in the church are recognized and selected by the members of the congregation largely due to the quality of their spiritual life and their pastoral gifting. Pentecostals place great importance on one's sense of a call, spiritual gifting, and ministerial practice. They resist bureaucratic control, fearing that it will limit Spirit-inspired vision. New churches are often birthed spontaneously, planted

---

141 Yonggi Cho, *Salvation,* 39.

142 Ulrich Luz, "Paul as Mystic," in *The Holy Spirit and Christian Origins: Essays in Honor of James D. G. Dunn,* eds. G. Stanton, B. Longenecker, and S. Barton (Grand Rapids: William B. Eerdmans, 2004), 141.

by believers with little formal training who sense the Spirit leading them to "step out in faith." These spiritual entrepreneurs frequently work through family relationships or friendship networks, moved by a sense of calling and spiritual vision. They are encouraged to develop vision and take risks through their participation in the life of the church. There is a strong egalitarian sense in the Pentecostal community, with every one encouraged to contribute. This is, of course, facilitated by an emphasis on gifts of the Spirit and symbolized in speaking in tongues, which can be viewed as a sacrament that is not limited to or controlled by the clergy.

By way of contrast, churches that are highly institutional and tightly structured do not tend to encourage or nurture the charismatic dimension. A key reason for this has to do with the way leaders are selected and how services are conducted. Churches that select leaders on the basis of their training and their standing within the institution are often unable to make room for many spiritually qualified and gifted leaders.

> **Pentecostals do not hesitate to relate the gospel to the whole spectrum of human need, whether it be spiritual, physical, or material.**

The more rigid the selection process, the harder it is to make allowance for gifted leaders who do not fit the normal pattern. This problem is clearly illustrated in the government-sanctioned church of China (TSPM),[143] where the process for becoming an ordained minister is very narrowly defined.

---

143   TSPM stands for "The Three Self Patriotic Movement."

A prospective minister must, above all, study at a TSPM seminary. This is tremendously limiting since educational levels in the countryside are often too low for admission, the prospective student must have recommendations from a TSPM pastor and thus prior experience in a TSPM church, and the number of students admitted into TSPM seminaries each year is ridiculously low due to government restrictions. After graduation, the young believer often serves an apprenticeship in a designated church under designated leadership. Given the mixed character of the TSPM, this can be a most challenging experience for earnest young believers. Finally, the ministerial candidate must be viewed as acceptable by both church and government leaders in order to be ordained.

With these factors in mind, we can understand why so many gifted young believers gravitate to house church settings. Here is an environment where they can exercise leadership gifts without going through a rigorous process that in most cases is not open to them anyway. Many opportunities to explore and develop their sense of calling are available in small group settings. And, while underground training opportunities are increasingly available to house church Christians, strong emphasis is placed on practical ministry. This tends to foster and strengthen the development of spiritual gifts. In the house church, anyone may emerge as a leader. The only qualifications are spiritual in nature.

It is important to note that TSPM churches tend to be dominated by the clergy. They do not feature participation or ministry on the part of the laity. If possible, the Sunday worship services are always led by professional clergy. Furthermore, small group meetings where lay leadership might be encouraged and developed are often not tolerated. Meetings must take place at designated places, at designated times, and with designated leadership. This limitation seriously impacts the life of the church, for these are precisely the contexts where gifts of the Spirit might be exercised and the body built up.

Of course the house churches are extremely different. Virtually everyone participates and anyone may contribute a song, a testimony, or a prayer. When I attend TSPM churches I am always encouraged, but generally I know that I will not be an active participant in terms of edifying the larger group. When I attend a house church service, I always go with a sense of expectancy, knowing that I will have many opportunities to share, to pray, and to encourage others.

These contrasts are not unique to the churches of China. Many traditional and state churches around the world insist that their ministers go through a rigid path of professional training. They also emphasize a clear path of hierarchical authority that features accountability. This kind of institutional approach may foster stability, but it also encourages conformity and stifles flexibility, creativity, and risk-taking. Fundamentally, the ministry is often viewed differently: it is seen as a profession to pursue rather than a calling to follow.

The ethos of Pentecostal churches is noticeably different. We may sum up by saying that Pentecostals are the "free market capitalists" in the economy of church life. Rigid control from a central bureaucracy is rarely tolerated; rather, the calling, gifting, and vision of every believer is affirmed and encouraged. Churches are thus planted with little or no encouragement or financial support from denominational leaders, often by surprising people —it matters not if they are young, unschooled, or female—with a strong sense that God has called and empowered them for the task at hand. Little wonder that Acts 4:13 is a favorite Pentecostal text: "When they saw the courage of Peter and John and realized that they were unschooled, ordinary men, they were astonished and they took note that these men had been with Jesus." Pentecostals see this life-transforming encounter with Jesus as the essential ingredient for effective ministry. Since other qualifications fade into insignificance by comparison, everyone is potentially a pastor, evangelist, or missionary. The church is, after all, a community of Spirit-inspired prophets.

> **Everyone is potentially a pastor, evangelist, or missionary. The church is, after all, a community of Spirit-inspired prophets.**

Many will point to the obvious risks inherent in this rather loose approach to church structure. An emphasis on strong, visionary leaders easily can lead to "apostolic" authoritarianism.[144] This danger is somewhat mitigated by the emphasis on the gifts and calling of every member in the congregation. However, tensions between strong leaders can often lead to church splits. What about the obvious potential for schism? This is certainly a natural and perhaps inevitable consequence of this more organic, charismatic approach to church life. Yet this weakness also contains within it an important strength. While churches tend to become more bureaucratic over time, the seeds for renewal are always germinating and ready to burst forth into fragrant life. As Martin notes, "For each instance where enthusiasm cools into settled forms and rationalization, there are

---

144   In his book on the Charismatic movement in Britain, Nigel Scotland chronicles a litany of problems related to authoritarian tendencies in church leadership. Although past extremes appear to have sobered the movement and much progress has been made, the abuse of "apostolic" authoritarianism is clearly a key concern for the future (*Charismatics and the Next Millennium: Do They Have a Future?* [London: Hodder & Stoughton, 1995], see chapters 4 and 5).

others which break the moulds, above all in the huge population of the non-western world."[145]

5. AN EMPHASIS ON EXPERIENCE

Although Pentecostals have always been people of the Book and committed to the Bible, they have also been quick to emphasize that the same experiences that shaped the life of the early church are available today. The New Testament church represents a model for their life and ministry, and this includes their experience of God. As the narrative of Acts reveals, the apostolic church was marked by powerful experiences that generated remarkable courage and intense emotions. How else do we explain the courageous witness of Peter and John (Acts 4:8–20) or the remarkable tranquility and compassion of Stephen (Acts 7:60)? How else do we explain the visions, the joy, the ecstatic praise, and the unwavering conviction that Jesus is alive? The early Christians were gripped by their experience of God.

Many in the modern era shied away from the enthusiasm of the apostolic church, viewing it as a primitive and relatively uncouth response to religious truth. They felt that enlightened and civilized people should respond in a more cognitive and serene manner. But none of this dissuaded Pentecostals from embracing the biblical record and seeking a profound encounter with God in Christ through the Holy Spirit. This approach has enabled the Pentecostal movement, at least in modern times, to bring together an emphasis on experience with a commitment to the authority of the Bible. Rather than seeing these twin themes as competing with one another, most Pentecostals view them

---

145   Martin, *Pentecostalism,* 176.

as complementary. Certainly, Pentecostals would affirm the importance of a cognitive grasp of basic, fundamental truths. Thus, Pentecostals have established thousands of Bible schools around the world. However, Pentecostals do not tend to look to creeds or doctrinal statements for a verification of true faith. A cognitive understanding of doctrinal truth may be helpful and even necessary, but it is not proof of spiritual vitality. Rather, Pentecostals see fervent prayer, a willingness to suffer for the gospel, and a deep sense of God's leading as signs of true spiritual life. Pentecostal theology is, at its heart, a theology of encounter.[146] Pentecostal doctrine—with its emphasis on baptism in the Spirit, speaking in tongues, and gifts of the Spirit—and Pentecostal praxis reflect this reality.

This positive and welcoming attitude toward experience marks Pentecostal services around the globe. Pentecostal meetings, although generally following a simple pattern of singing, preaching, testimonies, and prayer, nonetheless are often punctuated by manifestations of the Spirit and frequently end with an extended time of corporate prayer. The manifestations of the Spirit might take the form of a word of prophecy, a message in tongues (which is then interpreted for the congregation), or a word of encouragement. Most services end with an altar call "so that the goal of the preaching can be sealed with a season of prayer."[147] This time of prayer is viewed as the true climax of the service and an important opportunity for people to encounter God in a personal and tangible way. At this time special needs may be voiced. When a request for prayer is offered, the individual is frequently surrounded by a group of supportive intercessors

---

146   Keith Warrington, *Pentecostal Theology: A Theology of Encounter* (London: T & T Clark, 2008), 21.

147   Menzies and Menzies, *Spirit and Power,* 185.

who, with the laying on of hands, cry out to God on behalf of the person in need. Routinely, the sick are anointed with oil and prayer for healing is offered. Those struggling with temptation or addictions may be bathed in prayer as well, with the prayer extending until there is a sense of spiritual breakthrough or victory. Although this dynamic and participatory type of worship service is perhaps less common in the large Pentecostal churches of the West, generally even in these churches one can find a small group setting where these kind of experiences are encouraged and nurtured. It all makes for an interesting and exciting time. Pentecostal services are rarely dull.

In a world filled with people who long to experience God, to feel His presence, and encounter Him at a deeply personal and emotional level, this kind of dynamic worship service is very attractive.[148] The largely cognitive and sedate approach of traditional churches fails to connect with these needs. In fact, for the many illiterate or semi-literate people who populate our planet, a cerebral approach is virtually incomprehensible. They desire to meet God: a God who is tangible, whose presence can be felt, and whose impact can be seen and heard—a God who has power over evil spirits and who can change lives. Pentecostals proclaim that this is the God who is revealed in Jesus. The contrast with the cold, liturgical formalism and largely cognitive orientation of the traditional churches is evident. Is it any wonder that Pentecostal churches are growing?

Some will still remain skeptical. They will ask: Is not this approach to church life, with its emphasis on ecstatic experience, emotional response, and spiritual power, filled with inherent

---

148   Scotland notes that whereas "Western evangelicalism was very much a one-dimensional affair in which the middle classes . . . looked for 'sound teaching,'" the charismatic movement, with its experiential focus has met a growing desire for "deeper emotional and spiritual satisfaction" (*Charismatics*, 24).

dangers? Might it not encourage us to feature emotionally manipulative methods and to focus on superficial matters? Yes, undoubtedly, there are dangers. However, there is more danger in an approach that fails to make room for the full range of human experience, including the emotions, in our encounter with God. I have observed that post-Enlightenment Westerners tend to be far more worried about "emotional excess" than their brothers and sisters in the East. As a result, they often do not allow significant room for the place of emotions in their spiritual encounters. Non-westerners delight in "feeling" God's presence. If the biblical record is to be our standard, then perhaps we in the West should take careful notice.

CONCLUSION

I have argued that Pentecostal church growth flows naturally from five characteristics that mark Pentecostal church life. Each of these characteristics may be traced to the distinctive way that Pentecostals emphasize and read the book of Acts. While Pentecostal churches adapt to the various settings and cultures in which they exist, these foundational characteristics transcend specific cultural settings. They are common to Pentecostal churches around the globe precisely because all of these churches share a common commitment to the Bible and, more specifically, to a preferential reading of Acts. In short, since Pentecostals view the early church as described in the book of Acts as their model, the narrative of Acts represents a powerful and cohesive force that shapes global Pentecostal praxis.

As we have noted, each of these characteristics entails a certain amount of risk. Bold proclamation of the gospel often leads to persecution. A focus on evangelism and discipleship may be ridiculed by a world that only values material prosperity and remains blind to the holistic impact of the gospel. The message that miracles of healing and spiritual deliverance accompany the in-breaking of God's reign may also be rejected by skeptics as unscientific and manipulative. A church that accepts leaders with limited theological training and strong vision clearly runs the risk of chaos and schism. And, finally, an emphasis on experience will often be criticized by the affluent and cultured as superficial and unsophisticated. There are many reasons why the traditional churches have chosen not to take the Pentecostal path. Yet Pentecostal churches, for the most part, have been able to navigate these risky roads. They have pursued the journey with joy and a strong sense of purpose. And they have succeeded.

Pentecostal churches around the globe . . . share a common commitment to the Bible and, more specifically, to a preferential reading of Acts.

Perhaps a key to the success of Pentecostal churches can be found in their willingness to take risks. Desperate people take risks. They have little to lose. Historically, Pentecostals have been people with little to lose. As a result, they have been desperate for God. Globally, the majority of Pentecostals still live on the wrong side of the tracks: they are the poor, the powerless, and the marginalized.[149] So, they are hungry for God. And so, too, they recognize that they are absolutely dependent upon Him. Pentecostals talk about God's power because they know that they

---

149 Martin concludes, "We have in Pentecostalism and all its associated movements the religious mobilization of the culturally despised, above all in the non-western world, outside any sponsorship whatever, whether of their own local intelligentsias, or of the clerical and secular intelligentsias of the West" (*Pentecostalism*, 167).

are weak. They pray for God's healing and deliverance because they have no other hope. They seek God's presence because only in Him do they find joy and peace. In a word, Pentecostals are desperate. And Luke's narrative reminds us that God loves to work in and through desperate people:

> He has brought down rulers from their thrones,
> but has lifted up the humble.
> He has filled the hungry with good things,
> but has sent the rich away empty.
> (Luke 1:52–53)

CONCLUSION

T he Pentecostal movement is recognized around the world as a powerful and dynamic force impacting the lives of hundreds of millions of people. It is changing the face of the Christian church. And in many cases, such as that of Korea, it is hard to overestimate its impact on the larger society. Yet, in spite of all of this, many still do not see Pentecostals as having much to offer theologically. It is a movement of experience, we are told, not doctrine. In this book I have sought to challenge this faulty assumption. Pentecostals have an important theological contribution to make to the larger church world, if the other churches will simply listen.

First and foremost, Pentecostals are calling the church to take a fresh look at Luke-Acts. Only by hearing Luke's distinctive voice can we develop a truly holistic doctrine of the Holy Spirit. Only by reading Luke-Acts on its own terms can we understand the significance of the promised baptism in the Holy Spirit (Acts 1:5). For far too long, Protestant theology has highlighted Paul's important insights into the work of the Spirit, but largely ignored Luke's contribution. In this regard, Pentecostals are calling for a new reformation.

One of the great strengths of this fresh reading of Luke-Acts is that it highlights the missiological nature of discipleship and the church. Luke reminds us that the Holy Spirit is all about inspiring praise and witness for Jesus, and the Spirit's vision knows no boundaries. Regardless of one's race, gender, class, or region, all are called to participate in God's great redemptive mission. And all have been promised power to fulfill this calling (Acts 1:8). Pentecostals are calling the church to recover its primitive power and its apostolic calling. The church is nothing less than a community of prophets who are called to bear bold witness for Jesus.

Another great strength of the Pentecostal approach to Luke-Acts is its simplicity. As I have noted, Pentecostals love stories. We identify with the stories that fill the pages of the Gospels and the book of Acts, and the lessons gleaned from these stories are easily grasped and applied in our lives. For Pentecostals, Acts presents clear models that are to be emulated and guidelines that are to be followed. Our analysis of Luke-Acts, though based on modern hermeneutical methods, vindicates this simple and straightforward approach. Luke's purpose is indeed to provide his readers with models for their mission, models for their lives and ministries as Christians. Their stories are our stories. Luke desired that his church would read his two-volume work in precisely this way.

Finally, this reading of Luke-Acts also highlights the importance and symbolic significance of experiences of the Holy Spirit that inspire speaking in tongues: they remind us of our experiential link to the apostolic church and our similar callings. Their experience is our experience; their calling is our calling. The truths that we have outlined here are not only understood, but they can be felt. Both cognitive understanding and experiences that touch the emotions are important; they inform and impact one another. As we have seen, speaking in tongues incorporates in a unique way both of these dimensions. It serves, in a sense, as a sacrament: it is an outward sign of a spiritual reality. As we read the book of Acts, we can more fully appreciate the true significance of this experience. The experience encourages us to affirm with conviction that "[We] have received the Holy Spirit just as [they] have" (Acts 10:47;

cf. Acts 19:2, 6). It also calls us to embrace our true identity in Christ as end-time prophets (Acts 2:17–18).

This important theological legacy, this uniquely Pentecostal contribution to the larger church, needs to be passed on and communicated. It not only needs to be communicated to the larger church world, but it must also be passed on from generation to generation within Pentecostal churches. For this reason, I have also argued that clarity on matters of doctrine—on what Pentecostals believe—is important for the church. To insist on clear definitions concerning what the term *Pentecostal* means or to discuss what Pentecostals actually believe is not some sort of arrogant, Western imposition. Quite the contrary, it is simply an attempt to meet the needs of the church—the global, Pentecostal church, to be more precise.

Three chapters in this book were originally written and presented as special lectures in Amsterdam, Hong Kong, and Taipei. In each instance, local believers invited me to come and speak about various aspects of Pentecostal theology. In Amsterdam, I was asked to present a Pentecostal perspective on baptism in the Holy Spirit (in dialogue with Reformed theology).[150] In Hong Kong, I presented a paper on Pentecostal hermeneutics at a symposium for a broadly Evangelical group of pastors and teachers sponsored by Ecclesia Bible College, an Assemblies of God Bible school.[151] Finally, in Taipei I was asked by the local Assemblies of God churches to present a paper on the role of tongues in the New Testament.[152] My point is this: Pentecostal churches in Holland, Hong Kong, and Taiwan all felt

---

150 This formed the basis of Chapter 2.

151 This formed the basis of Chapter 1.

152 This formed the basis of Chapter 3, although it was originally presented in Mandarin Chinese.

the need for further clarification concerning distinctive aspects of their doctrine. They asked me to present on these topics; they felt the need.

About a year ago, Brother Wang,[153] a young Chinese house church leader, contacted me. A friend of Brother Wang suggested that he call me because Wang is intensely interested in Pentecostal values and experience. Brother Wang is a vibrant Pentecostal believer, and he knows a lot about the early Pentecostal history in our Province. After this initial contact we began meeting every Saturday morning in order to study the Bible together and pray. One morning, after we had met together a number of times, Brother Wang asked me an important question. Although he is a house church pastor, Brother Wang is attending a TSPM Bible school due to his past connections with the TSPM. He has been frustrated by what he is receiving at the local TSPM seminary. He feels that the "post-denominational" curriculum, which describes various positions on theological topics (e.g., Lutheran, Presbyterian, etc.), is confusing for young students. He said that he felt the various positions, which appeared to him to be contradictory at times, left most students confused and bewildered. "They don't know what they should believe," he stated.

> There are a host of earnest, dedicated young believers around the world who want to know what it means to be Pentecostal.

So, during our meeting he asked, "Can you help me understand Assemblies of God doctrine? I want to know what Pentecostals believe." The question was revealing, and it flowed

---

153   I am using a pseudonym to protect this man's identity.

from a real sense of need. Brother Wang yearns for a tradition, a clear and consistent body of doctrine to base his ministry upon. He is committed to Pentecostal doctrine, and he feels he doesn't get much encouragement in this regard at the TSPM seminary.

Brother Wang is not unique. There are a host of earnest, dedicated young believers around the world who want to know what it means to be Pentecostal. I pray that contemporary Pentecostals will be faithful stewards of the important theological legacy that we have received. I pray that we will pass on the message that was given a global voice at Azusa Street over a century ago. Their story is our story, and it is a story worth telling.

APPENDIX

William W. Menzies: A Pentecostal Life

By his sons Glen W. Menzies and Robert P. Menzies

William W. Menzies (July 1, 1931–August 15, 2011) was well known in Pentecostal circles as an educator, historian, and theologian. He was also a missionary, and the two poles of the latter decades of his life were Springfield, Missouri, where he lived on-and-off for more than fifty years; and Baguio City, the Philippines, where he served as President and Chancellor of Asia Pacific Theological Seminary (APTS). Over the course of his career he taught in a full-time capacity or served as an administrator at five institutions of higher learning: Central Bible College (1958–1970), Evangel University (1970–1980), the Assemblies of God Theological Seminary (1974–1984), California Theological Seminary (1985–1987), and APTS (President 1989–1996; Chancellor 1996–2011). He was the author of nine books and numerous articles, and among his most important accomplishments was the founding, along with Vinson Synan and Horace Ward, of the Society for Pentecostal Studies (SPS). He also served as the first President of the SPS and the first editor of its journal, *Pneuma*. To us he was simply "Dad."

"Bill," as his friends called him, was born in New Kensington, Pennsylvania. He was born to William E. and Sophie B. Menzies, and he was named after his father. His parents always called him "Junior."

William Sr., our grandpa, had earned a degree in electrical engineering from Penn State, and he spent much of his life engaged in both engineering and church planting. He would work for a while in engineering and save up some money. Then he would quit his job and build a church building. Grandma would play her trombone, both Grandma and Grandpa would preach, and when they got enough people coming to support a regular pastor, they would turn the church over to the new pastor and Grandpa would go back to engineering and saving up money. Eventually, the family moved to Dayton, Ohio, which is really where our dad grew up.

One of Dad's teenage passions was ham radio, and he continued to hold an amateur radio operator's license until the day he died. He fiddled with receivers, transmitters, matchboxes, and antennas. Glen remembers him telling a story about a neighborhood friend who also loved to work on things, including ham gear. Unfortunately, this friend's parents would not let him own a screwdriver. They wanted him to grow up to earn a living with his head, not his hands. So this friend would sneak over to Dad's place whenever he needed to use a screwdriver.

Dad's first ham radio transmitter was a used model he found at the very attractive price of twenty dollars. Apparently he did not have twenty dollars in cash at the time, so he convinced his mother to let him get the transmitter and even to help him finance the purchase. She was impressed with all of the research he had done on transmitters and what they cost, and she became convinced he had located a good deal. What he did not tell his mom was why the transmitter was available. Apparently the previous owner had been electrocuted by it. If his mom had known that, she never would have let him buy such a deadly machine. However,

Dad put a "bleeder resister" across the big can condenser that had killed its owner, making it much less of a hazard.

These stories explain something important about Dad. His attitude was: Why not be good with both your head and your hands? Dad was not interested in either mindless labor or in abstract theory that never connected with real life. He appreciated good theology, but good theology for him also meant that it impacted the life of the church.

When Dad graduated from high school he planned to become an engineer like his father. He enrolled at Ohio State. Somehow, he quickly sensed that this was not what God wanted for him, and he soon transferred to Central Bible Institute (CBI) in Springfield, Missouri, feeling that God had placed a call to ministry on his life.

Dad distinguished himself in school, earning extremely good grades. Elmer Kirsch, a friend and classmate, remembers him as a "brilliant" student. Another schoolmate from those years once complained to Glen that Dad had often set the curve, making the classes rougher on him than they would have been otherwise. During Dad's last year at CBI he was layout editor of the yearbook, and he was chosen as class speaker.

At Dad's funeral we were both surprised to learn that Dad had sung in the male chorus at CBI, since we never thought of him as being very musical. We also learned that one of his roles was as a "publican"—an official of the junior class who was charged with collecting class dues. We wish we had known about this earlier. As we were growing up we could have made good use of this, teasing Dad about being a "publican and sinner."

One of the more colorful activities Dad got involved in during his CBI days was the outstation ministry at Bald Knob, in the center of Ozark "hillbilly" country. The plan was to plant a church in a one-room schoolhouse. The school had no electricity, but there was a gas lamp hanging from the ceiling.

At that time there was an active feud between two of the families in the area, so some carried guns to the schoolhouse. Also, one gentleman wanted to attend services, but he was afraid to come on his own. He would attend if one of the CBI students would pick him up, because he was quite sure no one would shoot him while he was with a "reverend."

There was opposition to proclamation of the gospel at the Bald Knob School. Someone cut the brake lines on Elmer Kirsch's car, and it was only divine providence that kept several of the CBI students from dying in a car plunge from one of those old Ozark switchback roads that were so common in the early fifties. Elmer used the emergency brake to get back to CBI.

Despite the opposition, the work prospered and a church of about sixty people was established. Then came the event that ended it all. The wife of the Sunday School Superintendent plotted with a neighbor—who also attended the church—to kill her husband. The bloody deed was done with a pitchfork in the Sunday School Superintendent's barn. There was little law at that time in Taney County, since the sheriff had been run out of town and the deputy had quit lest a similar fate befall him. They finally were able to get a sheriff from Greene County to come down and arrest the murderer. The moral stain from these events, however, pretty well killed the CBI out-station efforts at Bald Knob.

Following Dad's graduation from CBI, he decided to attend Wheaton College near Chicago in order to obtain a four-year college degree and a Master's degree. It was in those years that he met Doris Dresselhaus, a farm girl from northern Iowa. Their first date took place in the basement apartment of Bob and Eilene Cooley. Eilene cooked a special spaghetti meal and no doubt the food was a hit. There is also no doubt that Mom was a bigger hit with Dad than the food. Soon they were married.

After three years of pastoring in Michigan, and the addition of two incredibly handsome young boys to their home, Dad was asked to return to CBI as a teacher. The year was 1958. Although money was scarce and Dad worked extremely hard, those were some of the happiest years of their lives.

In 1962 Dad began a two-year leave of absence from CBI so he could take doctoral classes at the University of Iowa. His program was in American Church History, and eventually he began work on the history of the Assemblies of God.

When Dad was preparing for his oral exams at the University, Bob was a five-year-old. Little "Bobby"—as he was called in those days—was impressed by a story Dad told of a man who had fainted during his doctoral examinations. So late in the afternoon on the day of Dad's oral exams, as he returned home from this grueling ordeal, Bobby rushed to the door to meet him, crying out, "Did you faint, Daddy?" Bobby was greatly relieved to learn that his dad had not fainted, and in fact, things had gone quite well.

After returning to Springfield and to CBI in 1964, Dad began serious work on his dissertation. Summers were devoted to traveling the country to interview important figures in Pentecostal history. Since the cost of staying at hotels was prohibitive for our family, Dad purchased a small camper that he hauled all over the United States. Those summers were incredibly interesting. When Dad was off interviewing, Mom and her boys would play in some scenic campsite. On the days Dad was free, we would tour battlefields or historic buildings or national parks.

We were always very proud of our dad, a fact that is illustrated by this little story. Back in the mid-1960s our family was driving through the Western part of the United States. We came to a narrow bridge just as a large earth-moving machine was slowly plodding across. Dad attempted to pass the machine and miscalculated, sideswiping one side of the bridge. It was a scary moment, with the car sliding and tires screeching. When the dust settled, Bobby's small, six-year-old voice broke through the silence, "Dad, I wasn't very proud of you back there." Mom and Dad broke into laughter, which did a lot to reassure us that everything was all right. That was perhaps the only moment in his eighty years that either of us was not proud of Dad.

When Dad's dissertation was completed and his degree conferred, we might have expected his scholarly activity to slow down a bit. Instead, it started all over again. The General Council leadership asked Dad to expand his dissertation into a more comprehensive history of the Assemblies of God. This required more interviewing and more traveling, but we did not mind a bit. More research meant more traveling and camping. Finally, in 1971, Anointed to Serve was published.

In 1970 Dad announced his decision to move across town to teach at Evangel College. One would think this would not have been a big deal, but this simple decision by a lowly professor produced a huge amount of controversy. Glen remembers, when he was about fourteen years old, being confronted near the entrance to Central Bible College (the new name of Central Bible Institute) by someone who felt the need to explain, "You know, your father is a traitor!" Glen responded, "Then maybe you ought to talk about that with him instead of me." If only Glen had had the gift of prophecy and could have replied, "It doesn't matter much that my dad is moving from CBC to Evangel because in forty years those two schools are going to merge anyway!"

Dad spent a decade teaching at Evangel, during most of which he also served as the Chairman of the Department of Biblical Studies and Philosophy. During that time two of his students were his sons. These, too, were happy years.

As teenagers, we boys always felt we had a sacred responsibility to keep Dad humble. Dad was not a social or professional "climber." Although he always dressed nicely—Mom saw to that—he was never overly concerned about his clothes. In this sense he was a child of Azusa Street; he lived simply and did not attempt to stand out. He was not a self-promoter. Generally, his clothes were neat, conservative, and simple. So whenever Mom did attempt to buy something new or in the slightest bit trendy, we took notice. When Dad came to the breakfast table wearing his new "fancy duds," we would break into a chorus: "Bill Menzies goes mod." These were the days when "The Mod Squad" was a popular TV show.

It was during this time that Dad, along with Vinson Synan and Horace Ward, established an academic society designed to promote research among Pentecostals. Many will regard the founding of the Society for Pentecostal Studies, which today draws hundreds of scholars from around the world to its annual meetings, as one of Dad's signal achievements. Dad served as the first President of the society and as the first editor of *Pneuma*, the society's scholarly journal.

At this time there was a lot of distrust of scholarship and academic pursuits in the Assemblies of God. But somehow Dad was able to disarm these suspicions. He was able to do this largely because of his godly character, humble spirit, and encouraging manner. After meeting Dad, people would often think, "Well, I guess these scholars aren't all bad." Dad won people over, and in this way he helped change attitudes within the Pentecostal movement towards higher education and scholarship. In short, he paved the way so that others could follow.

Following his time at Evangel, Dad taught for three years at the Assemblies of God Theological Seminary, spent a year as Interim President at FEAST (the Far East Advanced School of Theology), and then two years as the Vice-President for Academic Affairs at California Theological Seminary.

Dad was famous for the triangles he often drew on chalkboards or whiteboards. The many ideas and relationships these triangles illustrated are beyond counting. But there was a great deal more to Dad's teaching than the way he packaged things. He was a firmly convinced Pentecostal, and he believed that Pentecostal identity must be grounded in theology, not sociology. Pentecostalism held an important insight into the nature of apostolic Christianity; it was not simply the disgruntled response of people living on the margins of society to their economic plight.

Dad was also a stickler for academic honesty. He did not like it when scholars or organizations intentionally fudged the truth. For instance, when Dad was preparing *Anointed to Serve*, his history of the Assemblies of God, he accurately pointed out that the Assemblies of God was strongly committed to pacifism—the refusal to participate in war—prior to World War II. He was asked to remove this from his book because this was viewed as "inconvenient" in the early 70s, the Vietnam War era during which the book was being prepared. Dad refused to shade the truth in this way, although he tried to find a more diplomatic way to get the basic message across. Dad himself was not a pacifist, but he thought it was important to tell the story accurately.

Dad believed the greatest blunder that the Assemblies of God—at least the American Assemblies of God—made during his lifetime was the way it ignored the Charismatic Movement, acting as if it wished the Charismatics would simply go away. Not only was this a failure to recognize the hand of God at work, the Assemblies of God forfeited the opportunity to provide leadership to a movement that needed leadership and stability. In the end, the Charismatic Movement had considerably greater impact on Classical Pentecostalism than Classical Pentecostalism had on the Charismatic Movement. It did not need to be this way.

While Dad was certainly a passionately committed Pentecostal, he rejected any sort of Pentecostalism that minimized the importance of either Scripture or Christ. Another way to say this is that his Pentecostalism was both bibliocentric and Christocentric. While Pentecostals think spiritual experience is important, Dad insisted that all spiritual experience must be judged by the standards of Scripture. He was also skeptical of any emphasis on the Spirit that minimized the importance of Christ. Dad was not the sort of guy to look for parallels between Buddhist mysticism and Christian experiences of the Spirit. He believed the Holy Spirit was "the Spirit of Christ" and would always point to Him. Christ is the anchor that grounds any attempt to discern which spirits are of God and which are not.

In 1989 Dad became President of Asia Pacific Theological Seminary. For the preceding twenty years Dad had made summer trips teaching in various missionary settings, often in Manila or Seoul. So, in some ways his appointment at APTS was a natural extension of this part-time missionary activity. Apparently he had proven he had a missionary's heart.

Moving to the Philippines gave Dad a new jolt of enthusiasm and energy. He seemed to relish the challenges of cross-cultural ministry and leadership. Also, the fact that some of his students faced the very real prospect of imprisonment or martyrdom was a constant reminder of how much was at stake.

Prayer was a key to Dad's ministry. As young boys we remember often seeing him pace back and forth in our basement, calling out to God in prayer. Bob recalls borrowing Dad's Bible once and thumbing through the pages. As he did this, he came across a list of prayer requests. On a small piece of paper Dad had listed a number of items that formed the basis of his daily prayer. One item in particular stood out. He had written something like this: "Lord, help me care less about how other people view me and more about how you view me." That prayer clearly shaped Dad's life.

In 1996 our mother had a serious heart attack while in the Philippines and considerable damage was done to her heart. This heart attack effectively ended our parents' ability to live overseas. The damage to Mom's heart was so extensive that she was put on a transplant list, and in 1998 she received a new heart.

After Mom's transplant, Mom and Dad returned to Springfield and lived quiet but joyful lives in retirement until illness took them both. The last eight months of Dad's life were consumed by tending to Mom and spending time with her, a task he fulfilled joyfully. In many ways the care of old people for each other reveals a far deeper love than the passion of newlyweds.

We will always remember the way our parents loved each other.

BIBLIOGRAPHY

Anderson, Allan. *Spreading Fires: The Missionary Nature of Early Pentecostalism.* Maryknoll: Orbis, 2007.

———. *An Introduction to Pentecostalism: Global Charismatic Christianity.* Cambridge: Cambridge University Press, 2004.

———. "The Contextual Pentecostal Theology of David Yonggi Cho." In *David Yonggi Cho: A Close Look at His Theology and Ministry,* edited by W. Ma, W. Menzies, and H. Bae, 133–59. *Asian Journal of Pentecostal Studies Series* 1. Baguio: Asia Pacific Theological Seminary Press, 2004.

Berkhof, Hendrikus. *The Doctrine of the Holy Spirit.* Louisville: Westminster/John Knox, 1986.

Bock, Darrell L. *Acts.* Baker Exegetical Commentary on the New Testament. Grand Rapids: Baker, 2007.

———. *Luke.* The IVP New Testament Commentary Series. Downers Grove: InterVarsity Press, 1994.

———. *Luke 9.51–24.53.* Baker Exegetical Commentary of the New Testament. Grand Rapids: Baker Academic, 1996.

Büchsel, F. *Der Geist Gottes im Neuen Testament.* Gütersloh: C. Bertlesmann, 1926.

Bultmann, Rudolph. "New Testament and Mythology." In *Kerygma and Myth: A Theological Debate by Rudolf Bultmann and Five Critics,* edited by H. W. Bartsch, 1–44. New York: Harper & Brothers, 1961.

———. "αογαλλιάομαι" in *TDNT,* I: 19–21.

Calvin, John. *Institutes of the Christian Religion.* Two volumes. Translated by F. L. Battles and edited by J. T. McNeill. *Library of Christian Classics* 20. Philadelphia: Westminster Press, 1960.

Cho, David Yonggi. *Salvation, Health, and Prosperity: Our Threefold Blessings in Christ.* Altamonte Springs, FL: Creation House, 1987.

———. *The Fourth Dimension: The Key to Putting Your Faith to Work for a Successful Life.* Plainfield: Logos, 1979.

———. *The Fourth Dimension, Volume Two: More Secrets for a Successful Faith Life.* Plainfield: Bridge Publishing, 1983.

Conzelmann, Hans. *Acts of the Apostles.* Philadelphia: Fortress Press, 1987; German original, 1963.

Cox, Harvey. *Fire From Heaven: The Rise of Pentecostal Spirituality and the Reshaping of Religion in the Twenty-first Century,* 1995. Reprint, Cambridge, MA: Da Capo Press, 2001.

Dunn, James D. G., *Baptism in the Holy Spirit.* London: SCM Press, 1970.

_____. "Baptism in the Spirit: A Response to Pentecostal Scholarship." *Journal of Pentecostal Theology,* 3 (1993): 3–27.

_____. *Jesus and the Spirit: A Study of the Religious and Charismatic Experience of Jesus and the First Christians as Reflected in the New Testament.* London: SCM Press, 1975.

Ellis, E. Earle. *The Gospel of Luke,* revised edition. New Century Bible Commentary. Grand Rapids: Wm. B. Eerdmans, 1974.

Evans, Craig. *Luke.* New International Biblical Commentary. Peabody: Hendrickson, 1990.

Everts, Jenny. "Tongues or Languages? Contextual Consistency in the Translation of Acts 2." *Journal of Pentecostal Theology* 4 (1994): 71–80.

Fitzmyer, Joseph. *The Gospel According to Luke* (X–XXIV). The Anchor Bible, Volume 28A. New York: Doubleday, 1985.

Green, Joel B. *How to Read the Gospels and Acts.* Downers Grove: InterVarsity Press, 1987.

_____. "Learning Theological Interpretation from Luke." In *Reading Luke: Interpretation, Reflection, Formation,* edited by Craig G. Bartholomew, Joel B. Green, and Anthony Thiselton, 55–78. *Scripture and Hermeneutics Series* 6. Grand Rapids: Zondervan, 2005.

_____. *The Gospel of Luke.* The New International Commentary on the New Testament. Grand Rapids: Eerdmans, 1997.

Gunkel, Hermann. *The Influence of the Holy Spirit: The Popular View of the Apostolic Age and the Teaching of the Apostle Paul.* Translated by R. A. Harrisville and P. A. Quanbeck II. Philadelphia: Fortress Press, 1979.

Hacking, Keith J. *Signs and Wonders Then and Now: Miracle-Working, Commissioning and Discipleship.* Nottingham: Apollos/InterVarsity Press, 2006.

Haya-Prats, Gonzalo. *Empowered Believers: The Holy Spirit in the Book of Acts.* Translated by Paul Elbert and Scott A. Ellington. Eugene, OR: Cascade Books, 2010.

Hengel, Martin. *Acts and the History of Earliest Christianity.* Translated by J. Bowden. London: SCM Press, 1979.

Jellicoe, Sidney. "St Luke and the 'Seventy (-Two)." *New Testament Studies* 6 (1960): 319–21.

Jenkins, Philip. *The Next Christendom: The Coming of Global Christianity.* Oxford: Oxford University Press, 2002.

Luz, Ulrich. "Paul as Mystic." In *The Holy Spirit and Christian Origins: Essays in Honor of James D. G. Dunn,* edited by Graham N. Stanton, Bruce W. Longenecker, and Stephen C. Barton, 131–43. Grand Rapids: William B. Eerdmans, 2004.

Macchia, Frank D. "Astonished by Faithfulness to God: A Reflection on Karl Barth's Understanding of Spirit Baptism." In *The Spirit and Spirituality: Essays in Honour of Russell P. Spittler,* edited by W. Ma and R. Menzies, 164–76. London: T&T Clark International, 2004.

Marshall, I. Howard. *The Gospel of Luke: A Commentary on the Greek Text.* New International Greek Testament Commentary. Grand Rapids: Eerdmans, 1978.

Martin, David. *Tongues of Fire: The Explosion of Protestantism in Latin America.* Oxford: Basil Blackwell, 1990.

_____. *Pentecostalism: The World Their Parish.* Oxford: Blackwell, 2002.

Menzies, Robert P. "A Review of Darrell Bock's Acts." *Pneuma* 30 (2008): 349–50.

_____ "A Review of Keith J. Hacking's *Signs and Wonders Then and Now: Miracle-Working, Commissioning, and Discipleship.*" *Evangelical Quarterly* 79 (2007): 261–65.

_____. "Complete Evangelism: A Review Essay." *Journal of Pentecostal Theology* 13 (1998): 133–42.

_____. *Empowered for Witness: The Spirit in Luke-Acts. Journal of Pentecostal Theology Supplement Series* 6. Sheffield: Sheffield Academic Press, 1994.

_____. "John's Place in the Development of Early Christian Pneumatology." In *The Spirit and Spirituality: Essays in Honour of Russell P. Spittler,* edited by Wonsuk Ma and Robert Menzies, 41–52. *Journal of Pentecostal Theology Supplement Series* 24. London: T&T Clark International, 2004.

_____. *The Development of Early Christian Pneumatology with Special Reference to Luke-Acts. Journal for the Study of the New Testament Supplement* 54. Sheffield: Journal for the Study of the Old Testament Press, 1991.

_____. *The Language of the Spirit: Interpreting and Translating Charismatic Terms.* Cleveland, TN: Centre for Pentecostal Theology Press, 2010.

_____. "The Sending of the Seventy and Luke's Purpose." In *Trajectories in the Book of Acts: Essays in Honor of John Wesley Wyckoff,* edited by Paul Alexander, Jordan D. May, and Robert Reid, 87–113. Eugene, OR: Wipf & Stock, 2009.

_____. "The Persecuted Prophets: A Mirror-Image of Luke's Spirit-Inspired Church." In *The Spirit and Christ in the New Testament and Christian Theology,* edited by I. Howard Marshall, Volker Rabens, and Cornelis Bennema, 52–70. Grand Rapids: Wm. B. Eerdmans Publishing, 2012.

Menzies, William W. and Robert P. *Spirit and Power: Foundations of Pentecostal Experience.* Grand Rapids: Zondervan, 2000.

Metzger, Bruce. "Seventy or Seventy-Two Disciples?" *New Testament Studies* 5 (1959): 299–306.

Miller, Donald E. and Tetsunao Yamamori. *Global Pentecostalism: the New Face of Christian Social Engagement.* Berkeley: University of California Press, 2007.

Montague, George T. *The Holy Spirit: Growth of a Biblical Tradition.* New York: Paulist Press, 1976.

Morrice, W. G. *Joy in the New Testament.* Exeter: Paternoster Press, 1984.

Nickle, Keith F. *Preaching the Gospel of Luke: Proclaiming God's Royal Rule.* Louisville: Westminster John Knox Press, 2000.

Nolland, John. *Luke 9.21–18.34.* Word Biblical Commentary 35B. Dallas, TX: Word, 1993.

Poloma, Margaret M. *Main Street Mystics: The Toronto Blessing and Reviving Pentecostalism.* Walnut Creek: AltaMira Press, 2003.

Ruthven, Jon. *On the Cessation of the Charismata: The Protestant Polemic on Postbiblical Miracles. Journal of Pentecostal Theology Supplement Series* 3. Sheffield: Sheffield Academic Press, 1993.

Schweizer, Eduard. "πνεῦμα." In *Theological Dictionary of the New Testament,* VI: 389–455.

Scotland, Nigel. *Charismatics and the Next Millennium: Do They Have a Future?* London: Hodder & Stoughton, 1995.

Sherrill, John L. *They Speak with Other Tongues.* New York: McGraw-Hill, 1964.

Stronstad, Roger. *The Charismatic Theology of St. Luke.* Peabody, MA: Hendrickson, 1984.

Synan, Vinson. "The Role of Tongues as Initial Evidence." In *Spirit and Renewal: Essays in Honor of J. Rodman Williams,* edited by Mark W. Wilson, 67–82. Sheffield: Sheffield Academic Press, 1994.

_____. *The Century of the Holy Spirit: 100 Years of Pentecostal and Charismatic Renewal.* Nashville: Thomas Nelson, 2001.

Tannehill, Robert C. *The Narrative Unity of Luke-Acts: A Literary Interpretation, Volume 1: The Gospel According to Luke.* Philadelphia: Fortress Press, 1986.

Twelftree, Graham. *People of the Spirit: Exploring Luke's View of the Church.* Grand Rapids: Baker, 2009.

Vinson, Richard. *Luke.* Macon, GA: Smyth & Helwys
    Publishing, 2008.
Walsh, Arlene M. Sanchez. "Whither Pentecostal Scholarship?"
    Books and Culture (May-June 2004): 34–6.
Warrington, Keith. *Pentecostal Theology: A Theology of Encounter.*
    London: T&T Clark, 2008.
Wenham, Gordon. *Numbers: An Introduction and Commentary.*
    Tyndale Old Testament Commentary Series. Downers Grove:
    Inter-Varsity Press, 1981.
Wesley, Luke. *The Church in China: Persecuted, Pentecostal, and
    Powerful. Asian Journal of Pentecostal Studies* 2. Baguio: Asian
    Journal of Pentecostal Studies Books, 2004.
Wimber, John and Kevin Springer. *Power Evangelism.* San
    Francisco: Harper & Row, 1991.
Witherington, Ben, III. *The Acts of the Apostles: A Socio-Rhetorical
    Commentary.* Grand Rapids: Eerdmans, 1998.
Zwingli, Ulrich. *Commentary on True and False Religion.* Edited
    by S. M. Jackson and C. N. Heller. Durham, NC: The Labyrinth
    Press, 1981.

ABOUT THE AUTHOR

Robert Menzies completed his PhD studies (New Testament) at the University of Aberdeen, Scotland, under the supervision of I. Howard Marshall in 1989. He has authored several books on the work of the Spirit, including *Spirit and Power: Foundations of Pentecostal Experience* (Zondervan, 2000), which he co-authored with his father. Dr. Menzies is an adjunct professor at Asia Pacific Theological Seminary in the Philippines and the Assemblies of God Theological Seminary in the US. He has taught at Bible schools and seminaries in the Philippines, Australia, Fiji, Indonesia, Malaysia, Japan, Russia, Holland, Korea, and the United States. For most of the past eighteen years Dr. Menzies, along with his wife and two daughters, has lived and served in China. Dr. Menzies is currently the Director of Synergy, an organization that seeks to enable rural village people in Southwest China to live productive and fruitful lives.

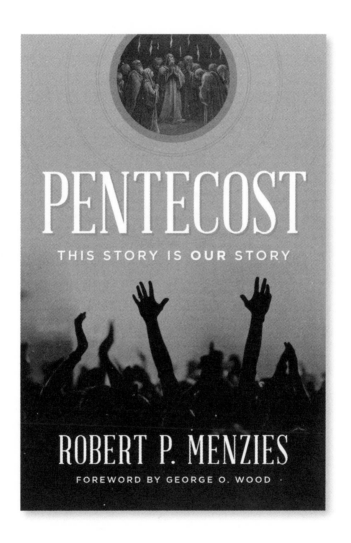

PENTECOST

THIS STORY IS OUR STORY

ROBERT P. MENZIES

FOREWORD BY GEORGE O. WOOD

For more information about this book
please visit **www.gospelpublishing.com.**